ReConnecting

A Wesleyan Guide
For the Renewal of Our
Congregation

ReConnecting

A Wesleyan Guide
For the Renewal
of Our Congregation

Rob Weber

Abingdon Press

ReConnecting: A Wesleyan Guide for the Renewal of Our Congregation

Participant's Guide and Daily Journal: ISBN 0-687-06535-6
Leader's Guide with DVD: ISBN 0-687-02234-2

This book is printed on acid-free, recycled paper.

04 05 06 07 08 09 10 11—10 9 8 7 6 5 4 3

MANUFACTURED IN THE UNITED STATES OF AMERICA

For my parents, Ted and Mudie Weber,
who connected me with the richness of life, history, and family.

CONTENTS

Introduction

GETTING STARTED   8

USING THE LEADER'S GUIDE WITH DVD   12

Session 1

WHERE IN THE WORLD ARE WE? GETTING OUR BEARINGS   17

Session 2

COMING HOME: REDISCOVERING THE ROOTS OF THE METHODIST MOVEMENT   31

Session 3

GOING DEEP: DISCOVERING THE ROOTS OF AUTHENTIC SPIRITUALITY   45

Session 4

OUTSIDE THE GATES: GETTING TO KNOW THE CULTURES IN OUR CONTEXT   59

Session 5

CLEAR EXPECTATIONS: WE EACH PLAY A PART   73

Session 6

THE EMERGING CHURCH: UNCOVERING OUR ANCIENT FUTURE   87

Session 7

LET'S ROLL: LIVING OUT THE VISION IN OUR CONGREGATION   101

Getting Started

WHAT'S IT ALL ABOUT?

Reconnecting responds to the cries and questions about ways in which United Methodist churches can be more effective in this rapidly changing world, while remaining strong and even renewing a connection with our tradition and heritage. *Reconnecting* is a seven-week series designed for use with groups in congregations who desire to be faithful and growing at this important time in history.

Disney's *The Lion King* was a smash hit as a movie and as a play on Broadway. The story centers on Simba, a lion cub who is destined to become the king. Simba is forced to flee his home (the Pridelands) because his evil uncle, Scar, convinced him that he was in some way responsible for his father's death. Simba grows up in a foreign setting and gradually forgets that he was originally created to become king. One day, Simba has an encounter with Rafiki the baboon, a wise medicine-man character, who lures him deep into the forest by telling Simba that he knows where his father is. Simba, believing that his father is dead, follows the baboon and finally comes to a small pool of water surrounded by high grass. Rafiki tells him to look in the pool. Simba is disappointed when all he sees is his own reflection—but Rafiki tells Simba to "*Look harder...*" With a touch of the baboon's staff, the water stirs, and when the reflection comes back into focus, it is not his own reflection that he sees, but the reflection of his father. "*You see,*" says the wise baboon, "*He lives in you.*" The image in the water then speaks to Simba and tells him "*You have forgotten me and you have forgotten who you are.*" He reminds his son that he is destined to be so much more than what he has become. After his encounter with his father's reflection, Simba is changed, and he heads straight back to the Pridelands to defeat Scar and take his place as king. Simba re-connected with his identity and purpose, and it changed the direction and outcome of his life.

As Jesus begins his ministry, he too has an encounter with a pool of water. Immediately following his baptism, Jesus hears the words "*You are my beloved son, with whom I am well pleased.*" This encounter is a defining moment for Jesus. It is a moment that imprints on his mind and soul who he is and what his life is for. When we engage in ministry it is important to remember that our ministry emerges from who we are and who it is that we have been created to become. Directly following this defining moment, Jesus sets off into the wilderness for a period of preparation. He spends forty days in prayer, meditation and fasting. After his time of preparation, armed with a connection to his identity as God's child, and a clear sense of purpose and mission, he is able to embark on a ministry that changes the world. From time to time it is important that we rekindle that sense of memory and identity that provide us with a reminder of what it is that we have been created for.

ReConnecting is a seven-week journey designed to help individuals and congregations encounter a fresh sense of identity, memory, and place in God's story. It is not a "church program," but rather a journey to be shared. The videos are not a series of lectures, or "talking heads." Instead, video becomes an instrument for creating shared experience. Video storytelling, interviews, and on-location filming at many of the historical locations important to the birth of the Methodist movement allow the participants to travel together to different places and to hear different perspectives from a variety of church leaders and theologians. Through *ReConnecting*, participants will experience a new or renewed connection with their identity, purpose, and place in the ongoing story of God's transforming and redeeming work in the world.

How is it used?

The *ReConnecting* experience is adaptable for a variety of settings.

- It is helpful for use with congregations that have been in existence for many years and need to share an experience of remembering who they are for the purpose of renewal or revitalization. (Think about what the remembering did for Simba.)

- It is helpful for congregations that are preparing to discern or rekindle vision, or are about to embark on a long range planning process.

- It is helpful in training leaders in the congregation by providing a deeper understanding of identity, direction, spiritual disciplines, and the purpose of the church.

- It is helpful for developing small groups and small-group leaders.

- It is a helpful launching pad for a variety of different adult spiritual formation experiences: Bible studies, spiritual formation groups, or covenant disciple groups in the Wesleyan tradition.

- It provides postmodern seekers with an experiential entry point into connection with the personally and socially transforming life of the early Wesleyan movement.

- *ReConnecting* is suitable for use as a congregation-wide emphasis, a small group resource, or an individual devotional guide. Instructions for planning and implementing *ReConnecting* for churches in a variety of settings is available on the DVD, or by download at www.cokesbury.com.

What can we expect?

Several congregations participated as test groups as *ReConnecting* was developed. It was used in large, medium and small congregations. Some churches were new with a low average age, and some tested had almost 200 years of history. In each setting the congregations experienced a burst of excitement and energy that served to launch them forward in ministry.

Results

One of the churches which used *ReConnecting* as a congregation-wide experience during the fall, with approximately 150 adults participating, shared these results:

- Eight new individuals/couples signed up for small-group leader training.

- Six participants formed a task group to develop a new series of adult education opportunities to accompany the new worship service.

- Twenty participants expressed interest in participating in the new educational opportunities.

- A visioning taskforce was established to discern strategies and direction for the church.

- Fifteen participants requested a program to help them understand ministry according to spiritual gifts.

- Eighteen participants registered for Disciple Bible Study.

- Twenty-two participants registered for a spiritual growth group.
- A group was formed to assess what was necessary to facilitate developing ministries that would reach more effectively beyond the walls of the church.
- Interest was expressed in exploring the possibility of developing a second site for the church to enable more people to be reached and the church to grow in ministry, mission, and members.

Other Comments about ReConnecting

"It helped me understand what the Church is all about!" *Marty, age 28*

"Wow! So that's who we are. I'm glad to be part of a church that can help change my life and make a difference in the world." *Shane, age 31*

"I learned more about what it means to be a United Methodist Christian during *ReConnecting* than I have during my whole life as a church member." *Suzie, age 45*

"*ReConnecting* became the "buzz-word" at our church. People became excited about the future of our ministry. It was just what we needed." *Linda, age 46*

"I've gained a new perspective on ministry beyond the walls of the church and I can't wait to get involved." *John, age 47*

"Now I understand why some churches are developing new styles of worship in order to reach new generations of people." *Bob, age 72*

If you or your congregation are longing for something that will help create a climate of excitement, energy, purpose, passion and connection with the changing world and our changeless God, then get ready to begin this journey of reconnection.

LET'S BEGIN

Maybe you have felt this before...The padded bar shuts across your waist with a muffled metallic sound, and with a slight jerk, you begin to roll out of the station. Filled with tentative anticipation, you proceed towards the base of the first hill. The free-gliding train switches masters, from the gravity drawing it downward to the rickety-sounding chain that grabs hold and brings it up to the top of the hill. There, in one pregnant moment, you survey your future—twisted, fast, scary, exciting, and exhilarating. That moment is a moment of release. It is a moment of trust as well as fear. Somewhere in the midst of those feelings is the edge of life for which we are willing to pay dearly, over and over. It is a moment of giving up control, and yet being able to trust that, in the midst of the excitement, you will remain safe. In order to enjoy the ride, you must let go. As we prepare to embark on a journey together, I believe we may experience some of the same feelings. We will be taking a journey together through history and our rapidly changing society. We will be covering a lot of ground in a short period of time. This can be a time of joy and excitement. I anticipate that you won't merely hold on tight and endure, but that you will let go and enjoy the ride.

Through the process of *ReConnecting*, I pray that you will be able to trust the God who holds us even in the midst of the twists and turns of life. So climb in. Take a seat. Buckle up. Put your hands in the air and give yourself to the journey.

How to use this manual

This manual will be companion and guide as you journey through *ReConnecting*. It is designed to help you hear from God through the process of reading, reflecting, and journaling. The next seven weeks can be a great experience for you and your companions. This experience has the potential to help deepen the connection that you have with God and with the life of the Church. The potential effectiveness depends upon you and the willingness you bring to participate. If you approach the readings, the journaling, and the group sessions with openness of heart and mind, and an active willingness to seek God's will for your life and the life of the church, you will not be disappointed.

The readings are from three sources. Each day, you will encounter:

- God's Words through Scripture;
- Wesley's Words through excerpts from his sermons,[1] and
- Contemporary Words, commentary to help provide direction for journaling and meditation.

Give yourself enough time with the readings to let the thoughts of the biblical writers and Wesley begin to stir thoughts in you. What were the they facing in life as they wrote these words? Whom did they have in mind as an audience? How is my situation similar or different from that of the author? These were real people with a passion for God, much like you and me. Ask yourself, "What were they trying to communicate and what does it say to me?"

It is important to understand that the readings are not chosen to communicate information; they are chosen to aid in transformation. Rather than providing commentary on the readings, their interpretation is left to you. The second dimension of the workbook, journaling, will help facilitate that process.

Journaling may be a new experience for you. It may seem strange to have a blank page staring at you with no direction about what to write. There is, however, a reason that the book was developed in this way. Instead of reading the passages in order to respond to a particular set of questions, or to get the "right" answer, you have an opportunity to listen, reflect, and see how God might speak to you personally in your own unique situation.

As you reflect on what you have read, you might want to write a *prayer*. The prayer could be carefully written, or simply an outpouring of your thoughts. You might want to imagine yourself writing a *letter* to the author of the passage, to Wesley, or even to God. Your writing might be in the form of *questions* directed to God, Wesley, yourself, your church, or the people outside the walls of the church. What might God put in a letter to you or to your church? Be creative. Be thoughtful. Be honest. Make the serious effort and watch the way God will begin to communicate with you through your own writings.

Schedule time for your reading and reflection. Don't make the mistake of thinking that you can just fit it in somewhere. Follow the example of John Wesley and get "methodical" about your time with God. Put it on your calendar and stick to it. If you schedule your time as an appointment with God, you will find it more difficult to skip. I believe that there is a God, and that God has real interaction with people. God's activity is not just something that happened way back then but continues here and now...and if we believe that, then, here and now, through this time together, we can CONNECT!

Using the Leader's Guide with DVD

The *Participant's Guide and Daily Journal* provides group participants with daily readings on each session topic, and the daily journaling exercises invite them to connect the biblical and Wesleyan principles with their own spiritual journey and the life of their congregation. This same material is also included in the printed *Leader's Guide*. The *Leader's Guide* also includes a DVD-ROM that contains everything you need during the session—including music, video, and presentation slides—for leading the *ReConnecting* experience. The additional resources found on the DVD are:

- A video introduction to the series;

- Seven professional twenty-minute video segments for viewing in group sessions;

- Seven music tracks for use in group worship and centering;

- Printable leader's guide with directions for planning and implementing the *ReConnecting* experience;

- Additional text files for use in getting the word out through bulletins, newsletters, posters and mailings;

- Files for overhead transparencies or PowerPoint® slides for use in class presentation;

- Suggestions for strategic planning and visioning.

WHAT ARE THE ADDITIONAL RESOURCES ON THE DVD?

The following is a list of the folders included on the DVD and a brief description of the files contained in each:

Leader's Guide

The *Leader's Guide* is included on the DVD as a PDF file (**Leader's Guide.pdf**). To open this file, you will need to have Adobe© Acrobat© Reader installed on your computer. (See page 13 for instructions about installing Acrobat Reader.) The *Leader's Guide* contains step-by-step instructions for leading each of the seven sessions, as well as ideas for ways to plan and implement the *ReConnecting* experience in your particular setting. You may make copies of the guide for multiple leaders.

Publicity and Poster

Materials have been included to help you publicize the *ReConnecting* experience for your congregation. Several different sizes and formats of a *ReConnecting* poster can be found on the DVD. Display these posters throughout your church to advertise when and where you will be offering the program. We have given you both an 8.5 x 11 size and a 11 x 17 size, in both PDF and TIFF format. If you have Acrobat© Reader, you can open a PDF version, print it out, and use a marker to fill in date, time, and location information on the bottom portion. Or you can open one of the TIFF files in a graphics program like Adobe© Photoshop or Photoshop Elements and type in this information. You will be able to print out the 8.5 x 11 version on a high quality color printer, or you can take the larger size to your local printshop for a printout.

The **Publicity** folder contains examples of a brochure, letters, and a registration card to help you inform your congregation about this exciting program. These files have been included as Microsoft Word documents and can be easily customized.

(Files included in the **Poster** folder are: **poster small.pdf, poster large.pdf, poster large.tif, poster small.tif;** the **Publicity** folder includes: **brochure.doc, registration card.doc, letter1.doc, letter2.doc**)

PowerPoint® Slideshows

Each session includes a short slideshow to help guide your group time. These slides are included as part of the DVD interface—and can be played directly from the session sub-menu—and also as PowerPoint files. If your church has the ability to connect a computer to a projector, you might prefer to copy the PowerPoint file to your hard drive and customize it for your particular setting. You would then be able to show it from PowerPoint just as you do with other presentations. (Files included: **Session1.ppt** through **Session7.ppt**.)

Acrobat Reader

The installation program for Adobe Acrobat Reader 5.05 has been included on the DVD so that you may easily install this program on your computer if you do not have it or if you have an older version that will not open the PDF files included. To install the reader, simply double-click the appropriate file for your computer platform and follow the onscreen instructions (**ar505enu.exe** for Windows; **ar505enu.bin** for Macintosh.)

How Do I Access These Resources?

To access the *Leader's Guide* and additional materials on the DVD, you will need to place it in a computer DVD-ROM drive. To browse to these data folders in Windows, open **Windows Explorer** and find the *ReConnecting* disk icon. Double-click the DVD icon for a listing of the contents. (Be patient; it may take several seconds for the list to appear.) You may also use **My Computer** to get a listing of the data folders. However, you will probably need to right-click the DVD icon and choose **Explore** rather than double-clicking since this might cause the DVD to begin playing. On a Macintosh, simply double-click the *ReConnecting* DVD icon to view the contents of the disk.

Once you have located the file you need, either copy the file to your hard drive or double-click the file to open it from the disk. If you open the file from the disk, remember that manipulating the file this way may be slower than if you copy it to your hard drive.

Playing the DVD on a Set-top Player

Set-top DVD players are connected to a TV. If you have played a DVD motion picture previously, you will see that the *ReConnecting* DVD behaves in the same way. Once inserted, the disk will begin playing automatically and will first bring up the copyright screen, followed by the **Main** menu. To navigate through the DVD menus, use the **Up** and **Down** arrow keys on your remote to move the pointer to the menu item that you wish to play. After an item is highlighted, press **Play** to move to the next screen, advance a slide, or to begin playing an item such as a video, music, or a presentation slideshow. Clicking the **Title** button will take you to back to the very beginning of the disk.

Volume is also adjusted in the normal way for your DVD player. Other buttons on the remote, like **Fast Forward**, will allow you to quickly move through a video or jump to the next item on the screen.

DVD Player Navigation Tips:

Title/Top=Beginning or Root Menu

Menu=Up one level

Arrow Keys=Move through graphical navigation buttons

Forward/Reverse=Fast forward or rewind video or music track

Next/Previous/Skip=Advance through slides

Stop=Restart DVD

Play=Play video, music or slideshow; advance slide

RECOMMENDED SYSTEM REQUIREMENTS FOR WINDOWS:

- Windows 98 and higher (ME or higher recommended)

- At least 400 MHz processor; 600 or higher

- 64 MB of memory; 128 or 256 recommended.

- DVD drive with appropriate drivers and software

RECOMMENDED SYSTEM REQUIREMENTS FOR MACINTOSH:

- G3 processor; 350 Mhz

- OS 9 or higher

- At least 64 MB of memory; 128 or 256 recommended.

- DVD drive with appropriate drivers and software

Computer Navigation Tips:

Title/Top=Beginning or Root Menu

Menu=Up one level

Title=Back to Root

Root=Back to Root or previous menu

Subtitle=Back to previous menu

Return=Stop playing Centering music

Arrow Keys=Move through graphical navigation buttons

Forward/Reverse=Fast forward or rewind video or music track

Next/Previous=Advance through slides

Stop=Exit DVD

Each slideshow also contains the music for that session and will automatically begin playing the music once you reach the slide with the music credits on it. Sessions 4, 6, and 7 also include the lyrics to the song and the slides will automatically advance in sync with the music. To stop the music and return to the menu, simply highlight the **Play Centering Music** button again and click **Play.**

This particular DVD contains content on both sides. **Sessions One through Three** are located on **Side 1** and **Sessions Four through Seven** are located on **Side 2**. If you try to access one of the sessions from the session menu that is not located on the current side, a screen will appear that instructs you to eject the DVD from the player, turn it over, and begin playing again. (The DVD is labeled on the inner metallic ring.)

Many of the screens also have embedded graphical buttons, such as **Menu**, to help you navigate. Selecting the graphical **Menu** button will take you back one level in the menu structure, depending on where you are. For example, if you have the menu for Session One onscreen, selecting **Menu** will take you back to the main session menu, which lists all seven sessions. Selecting the **Back** or **Next** button will move you through the menus at the same level, which in this example are the individual session menus.

USING THE DVD ON A COMPUTER

If you have the capability to hook a computer with a DVD player to a projector, you may choose to use this method to display the video and music components for the sessions. Every computer will have a different type of proprietary software that comes with the DVD drive, and the controls on each will vary slightly. Many of the buttons on the software interface will act just like the buttons on a DVD remote, though there will be some variation. Using the up and down arrow buttons on your software remote will cycle through highlighting each of the buttons, functioning just as they do on a set-top DVD player. (**Up** and **Left** will move through the buttons clockwise; **Down** and **Right**=counter-clockwise.) Once you have highlighted the button you want, hit the **Enter** key to activate the button. The advantage, however, of the computer navigation over the DVD set-top player is your ability to use the mouse to easily select the item you want by clicking on it.

In general, clicking the **Menu** button will take you back one step: if you are simply in a menu, it will take you up one level to the previous one; if you are playing a video, it will stop the video and take you back to the Session sub-menu. You can also use the **Menu** button to exit out of a video or slideshow. Depending on where you are, you may have several choices when you click the **Menu** button. **Title** takes you back to the very beginning; **Root** takes you back to the previous menu (if this is your only other choice); or if you also have **Subtitle** as a choice, **Root** will take you back to the opening **Main** menu while **Subtitle** will take you back to the previous menu (usually the individual session menu).

Clicking the **Title** button will take you to back to the very beginning of the disk. The **Fast Forward** and **Rewind** buttons will allow you to advance or rewind the video. **Next** and **Previous** will only work to advance you through the slides in the slideshow.

Each slideshow also contains the music for that session and will automatically begin playing it once you reach the slide with the music credits on it. Sessions 4, 6, and 7 also include the lyrics to the song and the slides will automatically advance with the music. To stop the music and advance, you can simply click the **Next** button in Sessions 1, 2, 3, and 5 or **Menu > Root** in Sessions 4, 6, and 7.

Recommended Resources on Wesley

John Wesley on Christian Beliefs: The Standard Sermons in Modern English Vol. 1, 1-20, Kenneth Cain Kinghorn. ISBN 0-687-05296-3, $28.00.

John Wesley on the Sermon on the Mount: The Standard Sermons in Modern English Vol. 2, 21-33, Kenneth Cain Kinghorn. ISBN 0-687-02810-8, $28.00.

John Wesley: Holiness of Heart and Life, Charles Yrigoyen. ISBN 0-687-05686-1, $11.00.

Responsible Grace, Randy Maddox. ISBN 0-68700334-2, $24.00.

The Scripture Way of Salvation: The heart of Wesley's Theology, Kenneth J. Collins. ISBN 0-687-00962-6, $20.00.

Practical Divinity Volume 1: Theology in the Wesleyan Tradition, Thomas Langford. ISBN 0-687-07382-0, $25.00.

Practical Divinity Volume 2: Readings in Wesleyan Theology, Thomas Langford. ISBN 0-687-01247-3, $25.00.

A Wesleyan Spiritual Reader, Rueben P. Job. ISBN 0-687-05701-9, $15.00.

Rethinking Wesley's Theology for Contemporary Methodism, Randy Maddox. ISBN 0-687-06045-1, $24.00.

Wesley and the Quadrilateral: Renewing the Conversation, Stephen Gunter, Scott Jones, Ted Campbell, Rebekah Miles, Randy Maddox. ISBN 0-687-06055-9, $20.00.

A Real Christian: The Life of John Wesley, Kenneth J. Collins. ISBN 0-687-08246-3, $20.00.

Conversion in the Wesleyan Tradition, Kenneth J. Collins, John Tyson. ISBN 0-687-09107-1, $27.00.

The Wesleyan Tradition: A Paradigm for Renewal, Paul Chilcote. ISBN 0-687-09563-8, $24.00.

The New Creation: John Wesley's Theology Today, Theodore Runyon. ISBN 0-687-09602-2, $21.00.

John Wesley's Conception and Use of Scripture, Scott Jones. ISBN 0-687-20466-6, $20.00.

Wesley and the People Called Methodists, Richard Heitzenrater. ISBN 0-687-44311-3, $24.00.

The Works of John Wesley, Volume 24, W. Reginald Ward and Richard Heitzenrater, eds. ISBN 0-687-03349-7, $55.00.

John Wesley's Life and Ethics, Ronald H. Stone. ISBN 0-687-05632-2, $25.00.

Aldersgate Reconsidered, Randy Maddox. ISBN 0-687-00984-7, $17.00.

John Wesley's Sermons: An Anthology, Albert C. Outler. ISBN 0-687-20495-X, $22.00.

JW and Company. ISBN 0-687-81832-5, $79.95.

Happy Birthday, John Wesley. ISBN 0-687-51362-1, $6.50.

Visual Treasury of United Methodism. ISBN 0-687-72668-9, $17.00.

Hearts on Fire: The United Methodist Story, Student. ISBN 0-687-72796-0, $5.00.

Fired Up: Youth Living as United Methodists Today, Leader. ISBN 0-687-72797-9, $5.00.

Sermons and Hymns of John Wesley, Richard Heitzenrater. CD-ROM ISBN 0-687-03350-0, $47.20

The Works of John Wesley. CD-ROM ISBN 0-687-70922-1, $99.95.

Politcs in the Order of Salvation: Transforming Wesleyan Political Ethics, Theodore Weber. ISBN 0-687-316901, $35.00.

Endnotes

[1] Unless otherwise noted, quotations from Wesley were taken from *The Works of Wesley on CD-ROM* (Franklin: Providence House Publishers, 1995).

Additional Resources from Grace Community

RECONNECTING
A WESLEYAN GUIDE FOR THE RENEWAL OF OUR CONGREGATION

BY ROB WEBER

ReConnecting is a seven-week or seven-session experience designed to get congregational small groups in touch with historical (Wesleyan) roots and contemporary cultural forces, so that an individual can embrace his or her "priesthood." Also an envelope for a church vision and for strategic planning used throughout a congregation and based in prayer and identity formation. The use of the seven-session experience may be customized based on the churches' vision and need—to simulate a frozen congregation, to deploy as an adult group Lenten activity, or to revisit a Wesleyan heritage.

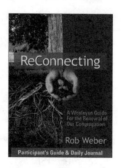

Leader's Guide
Publication Date:
10/2002
ISBN: 0-687-02234-7
Price: $39.00

Participant's Guide
Publication Date:
10/2002
ISBN: 0-687-06535-6
Price: $10.00

- Leader's Guide included on DVD as a PDF file (printed book contains text of the Participant's Guide)
- Promotional Video Trailer (a summary of the sessions).
- Customizable Poster (TIFF and PDF format)
- Publicity material (Sample letters, brochure, and registration card).

System Requirements:

DVD is compatible with all DVD set top players and most PC DVD-ROM players.
Participant's Guide does not include DVD.

Note to Leaders:
You will want to purchase a copy of the Participant's Guide for each group member. You will also need to purchase at least one copy of the Leader's Guide with DVD.

VISUAL LEADERSHIP
THE CHURCH LEADER AS IMAGESMITH

BY ROB WEBER

Rob Weber stresses the importance for a church leader in our current multisensory and multicultural society to lead through engaging people in the multisensory world of images. This kind of leadership requires skills in storytelling and media.

Publication Date:
10/2002
ISBN: 0-687-07844-X
Price: $15.00

The leader must develop sensitivity to a variety of media forms as well as an understanding of the multiple levels of story, understanding, and image out of which (and into which) people live. This book examines the process of a "visual" form of leadership in which these principles and the process can be applied in a variety of settings by allowing for enhanced communication and fostering the development of congregational ownership over vision and direction.

REKINDLING
A GUIDE FOR CONGREGATIONS WITH MULTIPLE OR ALTERNATIVE WORSHIP PATTERNS

BY STACY HOOD

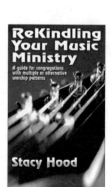

Whether your church is looking to add to a traditional music program or start a nontraditional music ministry, *ReKindling Your Music Ministry* provides worship leaders advice on making an effective transition into a new music format by reducing or better managing conflict. The "key" ingredient in a music ministry is to focus hearts on doing God's will—which is an excellent antidote to anxieties about entertainment and performance in worship.

$10 eBook available from Cokesbury.com in Palm, Abobe, and Microsoft formats.
(Click "eBooks & eDocs" tab.)

For more information about Grace Community Church, visit www.gracehappens.org.
For more information about Rob Weber, visit www.RobWeber.org.

1 WHERE IN THE WORLD ARE WE?

Getting Our Bearings

How can you know where you're going if you don't know where you are?

—*Caterpillar,* **Alice's Adventures in Wonderland**

WHERE IN THE WORLD ARE WE?

Getting Our Bearings

In the film *Patch Adams*, Robin Williams portrays a man who seeks help from the medical profession for his problems. In the mental institution to which he has committed himself, his experience with the doctor is less than helpful; however, he does discover his own passion for helping people overcome their problems. To this end he decides to enter medical school and become a doctor, but what he finds at medical school is not at all what he expects. In the first lecture, he hears that the goal of medical school is to remove the humanity from the students so that they can be more than human, so that they can become doctors.

Throughout the movie, we see an unfolding of the struggle between Patch's desire to help people and the structure of the medical profession that has become depersonalized. Patch constantly ignores the rules of the profession in order to spend time with the patients, aid in the process of healing, and improve the quality of life. When the authorities ban him from using unconventional methods in his hospital work, he looks beyond the current system and moves beyond its boundaries to start a free medical clinic, the "Geshundheit Institute." Here, the dichotomy between patient and doctor is blurred. Doctors provide care for the patients, but the patients are all expected to share in the care of one another as well. Patient thus becomes doctor. Some of the authorities in the medical system who see Patch's unconventional approach to medicine as a threat to their power try to block him from graduation. After a hearing, Patch is told that, while his methods are unconventional and somewhat threatening to the current system, a fire burns within him, a flame of passion for the life of the patient that could spread "like a brushfire" throughout the medical profession.

The story of Patch Adams and his struggle with the medical profession is an analogy to the life of Jesus and his encounter with the religious system of his day. The Judaism of Jesus' day was developed as a system to provide connection between people and God. It was a system of rules and relationships designed to provide for a whole and healthy community. This was the system into which Jesus was born and in which he was recognized as a rabbi. Yet Jesus encountered challenges in the system when he attempted to focus on the needs of the people at the expense of systemic regulations. The Pharisees watched and criticized him for healing on the

Sabbath, eating with the unclean, spending time with tax collectors and prostitutes, and asking people to look beyond the law to the humanity for which it was created. Eventually, as Jesus moved further beyond the accepted systemic boundaries and as the threat to the authority of those in power became greater, Jesus, too, was brought to a hearing, but instead of recognizing his innovations and people-centered ministry as positive, he was sentenced to death.

In both these situations, systems created originally out of good motives evolved to the point of being concerned more with the maintenance of the system itself than with the purpose for which the system was created. The systems that had been created with the good of the people at heart had evolved to the point that the professional practitioners of the systems were the focus rather than the care receiver and his or her needs. In both cases, the reformer who turned the focus back to the original motivation for the system, and who bypassed the rules and regulations that had been created, was ridiculed and forced to operate outside the system. This recurrent pattern can be seen in the religious reformations in the Christian Church throughout history, and I believe that the phenomenon of institutionalization and renewal has much to say to us as we consider the challenges facing the church in the third millennium.

A Time of Changes and Choices

Here at the beginning of the twenty-first century, we are experiencing a time of rapid change. Ours is an exploding information age. It is a postmodern time, a time that many have labeled as post-Christian. The context of change provides many challenges and opportunities for the church. We are at a crossroads, a turning point in the life of the church. We cannot pretend that this is a time for life as usual. We cannot go about the business of doing simply what we are used to doing. We are in danger. During the 1950s the mainline church in America experienced tremendous growth. Over the past twenty-five years, that trend has reversed and the church has experienced a time of rapid decline. Various responses to the crisis of decline have emerged, ranging from denial to church growth strategies, to the charismatic renewal movement. It is in the context of turbulence, flux, and shifting social orientations that we must focus on the challenges facing the church in the twenty-first century.

WHERE IN THE WORLD ARE WE?

God's Words

Remember the days of old; consider the generations long past. Ask your father and he will tell you, your elders, and they will explain to you.

—Deuteronomy 32:7 (NIV)

Wesley's Words

The First general advice which one who loves your souls would earnestly recommend to every one of you is: "Consider, with deep and frequent attention, the peculiar circumstances wherein you stand."

—"Advice to the People Called Methodists"

Contemporary Words

DAY 1

A young man who was in the Marines shared with me an experience he had in "survival training." He said that he was "dropped" in a heavily wooded, mountainous area that was unfamiliar to him. All he was given was a compass and a topographical map. With these two items, he was directed to find his way to the rendezvous point. The first thing he had to do was attempt to discern where he was so that he could begin his journey. Without knowing where he was, it would be impossible for him to chart a course to his desired destination.

There are times when it is important for each of us as followers of Christ to stop and look carefully at where we are in the wilderness of life so that we can plot a course toward faithful life in Christ. This is also true for congregations. As we begin this *ReConnecting* process, let us consider where it is that we find ourselves as individuals and as a church so that we can embark on the continued journey toward faithfulness.

———— Week One ————

My Words

Thoughts tend to become "untangled" when we pause to write them down. Take a few moments and reflect. Ask God to show you a picture of where you are in your life of faith. Are you at the beginning of your journey? Are you in full sprint toward the fullness of life for which God has created you? Are you stalled along the road for one reason or another? Are you wandering around, uncertain as to your direction?

After reflecting on your life, write a short letter to God describing what you see.

I see that I am not fulley devoted to god, But more so to my own life. But I try to be a good christan. But I do not Read god word. ore from his word. that well.

WHERE IN THE WORLD ARE WE?

God's Words

I remember the days of long ago;
I meditate on all your works and consider what your hands have done.
I spread out my hands to you;
   my soul thirsts for you like a parched land.

—Psalm 143:5–6 (NIV)

Wesley's Words

Is it not the common practice of the old men to praise the past and condemn the present time? And this may probably operate much farther than one would at first imagine. When those that have more experience than us, and therefore we are apt to think more wisdom, are almost continually harping upon this, the degeneracy of the world; those who are accustomed from their infancy to hear how much better the world was formerly than it is now, (and so it really seemed to them when they were young, and just come into the world, and when the cheerfulness of youth gave a pleasing air to all that was round about them,) the idea of the world's being worse and worse would naturally grow up with them. And so it will be, till we, in our turn, grow peevish, fretful, discontented, and full of melancholy complaints, "How wicked the world is grown! How much better it was when we were young, in the golden days that we can remember!"

—"Of Former Times," no. 102, 9

DAY 2

Contemporary Words

Frequently, as I visit with leaders and members of churches, I hear stories about fond memories of the past, when the world didn't seem so fragmented, and the challenges facing the church didn't seem so complicated and difficult. I hear stories of full buildings and of vitality of ministry and mission. "I remember when we built this building. The church was full, and there were children and youth everywhere. People just don't seem to come to church like they used to. These days, people seem to be too busy and preoccupied. I wonder what has happened to commitment to the church."

Wesley heard these concerns as well. It was as if the people in the church were interpreting their present situation in light of their memories of what the church had been like before. The decline in participation and activity led to a sense of despair and backward focus. When life is lived with backward focus, it is difficult to appreciate the possibilities and opportunities that exist in the present. Wesley called people to stop idealizing the past, and to begin looking at the present with eyes toward the future. Could this be such a time for us as well?

─────── **WEEK ONE** ───────

My Words

What are some of the greatest changes in the world that you have experienced in your life?

COMPUTERS
HIGHWAYS —ÖFAllon
CARS

How have those changes affected your life?

I cant go anywhere for traffic-
My work is more compleetox.

How have those changes affected the church?

Fewer people going I think
computer and Book work.
not so much are church.

WHERE IN THE WORLD ARE WE?

God's Words

Why do my people say, "We are free to roam; we will come to you no more"?
Does a maiden forget her jewelry, a bride her wedding ornaments?
Yet my people have forgotten me, days without number.

—Jeremiah 2:31–32 (NIV)

Wesley's Words

Was the last century more religious than this? In the former part of it, there was much of the form of religion; and some undoubtedly experienced the power thereof. But how soon did the fine gold become dim! How soon was it so mingled with worldly design, and with a total contempt both of truth, justice, and mercy, as brought that scandal upon all religion which is hardly removed to this day! Was there more true religion in the preceding century,—the age of the Reformation? There was doubtless, in many countries, a considerable reformation of religious opinions; yea, and modes of worship, which were much changed for the better, both in Germany and several other places. But it is well known that Luther himself complained with his dying breath, "The people that are called by my name (though I wish they were called by the name of Christ) are reformed as to their opinions and modes of worship; but their tempers and lives are the same as they were before."

—"Of Former Times," no. 102, 14

DAY 3

Contemporary Words

Travelers in Europe often visit a number of the great old cathedrals, the megachurches of an earlier era. These cathedrals stand as a testimony to the commitment, faith, and determination of those who spent their lives building them. The structures were built in prominent locations in each city or town. The architecture served to point heavenward and provide a setting in which people could feel awe and reverence in the presence of God. I notice, however, that many of these great buildings show little sign of life, and feel like memorials to a previous age. In many places throughout Europe, the church has experienced serious decline. What happened?

Some say that if you wonder about the future of the church in America, simply look to what has happened in Europe.

—————— WEEK ONE ——————

My Words

Imagine your world without the influence of the Church. What would it be like?

*Drinking, and Running around.
(High power)
missing out on God word.*

*Have some one to turn to.
in Need.*

Describe what that world would be like, paying attention to the feelings that accompany your description.

(To help me in prayer)

For answers.

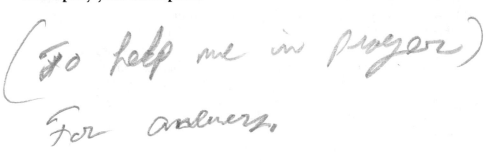

WHERE IN THE WORLD ARE WE?

God's Words

They devoted themselves to the apostles' teaching and to the fellowship, to the breaking of bread and to prayer. Everyone was filled with awe, and many wonders and miraculous signs were done by the apostles. All the believers were together and had everything in common. Selling their possessions and goods, they gave to anyone as he had need. Every day they continued to meet together in the temple courts. They broke bread in their homes and ate together with glad and sincere hearts, praising God and enjoying the favor of all the people. And the Lord added to their number daily those who were being saved.

—Acts 2:42–47 (NIV)

Wesley's Words

But between fifty and sixty years ago, a new phenomenon appeared in the world. Two or three young men, desiring to be scriptural Christians, met together for that purpose. Their number gradually increased. They were then all scattered. But fifty years ago, two of them met again; and a few plain people joined them, in order to help one another in the way to heaven. Since then they increased to many thousands, both in Europe and America. They are still increasing in number, and, as they humbly hope, in the knowledge and love of God; yea, and in what they neither hoped for nor desired, namely, in worldly substance.

—"Thoughts Upon a Late Phenomenon," no. 15

Contemporary Words

In the early 1700s, John Wesley embarked on a journey that changed the direction of the church. He emphasized a personal encounter with Christ and an experience of salvation. No longer was it enough to have a mental agreement with, or a belief in, Christianity. To be a Christian, one needed to be transformed into newness of life through a heart-felt relationship with the living Lord. The orientation of the church, which had become an institution maintained by and for the establishment, became directed towards those who were disenfranchised.

—————— **WEEK ONE** ——————

My Words

What is the difference between believing in Jesus and having a personal relationship with Jesus?

How do you experience salvation in your own life?

WHERE IN THE WORLD ARE WE?

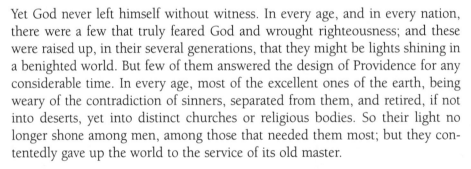

God's Words

Forget the former things;
    do not dwell on the past.
See, I am doing a new thing!
Now it springs up; do you not perceive it?
I am making a way in the desert
    and streams in the wasteland.

—Isaiah 43:18–19 (NIV)

Wesley's Words

DAY 5

Yet God never left himself without witness. In every age, and in every nation, there were a few that truly feared God and wrought righteousness; and these were raised up, in their several generations, that they might be lights shining in a benighted world. But few of them answered the design of Providence for any considerable time. In every age, most of the excellent ones of the earth, being weary of the contradiction of sinners, separated from them, and retired, if not into deserts, yet into distinct churches or religious bodies. So their light no longer shone among men, among those that needed them most; but they contentedly gave up the world to the service of its old master.

—"Thoughts Upon a Late Phenomenon," no. 3

Contemporary Words

Wesley's objective was "To reform the world and to spread scriptural holiness across the land." The movement that he started had a great and powerful effect on England and the budding nation in America. Over the years, Methodists have accomplished much as they sought to bring the touch of Christ to the lost and the disenfranchised. Wesley noticed, however, that in many instances, churches had become focused inward rather than outward so that the majority of the activities of the church were devoted to self-preservation rather than the original mission. This pattern is a natural pattern of institutional development, but unless the move toward inward focus is countered by a re-focusing on the original mission, then the institution will decline until it no longer exists.

─────────── **WEEK ONE** ───────────

My Words

Why does the church exist?

In the form of a letter, describe to God the main areas of mission and activity of your congregation.

NOTES

2 COMING HOME

Rediscovering the Roots Of the Methodist Movement

Therefore I intend to keep on reminding you of these things, though you know them already and are established in the truth that has come to you.

—2 Peter 1:12 (NRSV)

COMING HOME

Rediscovering the Roots of the Methodist Movement

I remember hearing someone tell about a family who had a son come home from Vietnam. It was a time of preparation and joy because he was returning and had not been killed. It was also an awkward time because while he was coming home and seemed in every way to be healthy and whole, just as when he had left, he had developed amnesia. He was coming home to the place of his childhood, yet he could not remember that childhood. He would come home to look into the faces of his mother, father, sisters, and brothers and know that at one time in his life they had been close, yet now, he didn't know who they were. The family knew that this was going to be a difficult time, but they also knew how important it is to be connected to family and memory. They decided to find everything they could that might help him relearn his family identity, his history, his memory.

Many of us may be in a similar situation when it comes to memories of the history and heritage of our faith. We haven't necessarily been "off to war," although some have, but we have been off in a "foreign land" of a rapidly changing culture. This week begins that process of *ReConnecting* with memory so that we will feel at home in our family of faith once again. As we look back, we will tap into a time wherein Wesley had the opportunity to share with his "flock" a "Readers' Digest version" of the history the people called Methodists.

On April 21, 1777, the foundation of Wesley's new church facility in London was being laid. On this occasion Wesley took time to reflect on the events that shaped the movement that became the Methodist Church. This week, we will use those reflections and remembering as the basis for our readings.

As we reconnect to the story of John Wesley, which is our own story and a part of our corporate memory, I believe that we, too, can capture a sense of that powerful faith and that passionate calling. I believe that it is possible for us to get a sense of the vision that drove Wesley to make disciples and to see scriptural holiness spread across the face of the earth. I also believe that if we allow ourselves to seek with open hearts and minds, the presence of God can and will be made powerfully real to us.

Over the next few weeks, we will look more deeply into some of the experiences, events, and outcomes of the process of living out this newfound faith and direction and the way these experiences shaped the church that has shaped us.

John Wesley's Formative Experiences

1) Family of Faith: He was raised by parents who understood the importance of the life of faith, and in this setting he was able to witness not only the message of the importance of faith but also faith and personal devotion lived out on a daily basis.

2) Hand of God: He had an experience of God's touch on his life and believed that in some way he had been set apart by God for a purpose. He was a "brand plucked from the burning."

3) Continuing Formation: He had a commitment to education and the practice of the spiritual disciplines and to being part of a mutual accountability group.

4) Life of Service: His faith was developed by and expressed in works of service and outreach.

5) Experience of Failure: He knew firsthand the experience of failure and the importance of trusting in God's grace. This allowed him to maintain an openness to new ideas and remain careful so as not to become so dogmatic that he could not change his mind.

6) Experience of Faith: His life was changed when his faith became experienced instead of just believed.

7) Reaching Out: His life and ministry became driven by the motion and direction found in living out the Great Commission.

COMING HOME

God's Words

Is not this man a brand plucked from the fire?

—Zechariah 3:2b (NRSV)

Wesley's Words

"Saved from the Fire"

Seeing the room was very light, I called to the maid to take me up. But none answering, I put my head out of the curtains, and saw streaks of fire on the top of the room. I got up and ran to the door, but could get no farther, all the floor beyond it being in a blaze. I then climbed up on a chest which stood near the window: One in the yard saw me, and proposed running to fetch a ladder. Another answered, "There will not be time; but I have thought of another expedient: Here, I will fix myself against the wall; lift a light man, and set him on my shoulders." They did so, and he took me out of the window. Just then the whole roof fell in; but it fell inward, or we had been all crushed at once. When they brought me into the house where my father was, he cried out, "Come, neighbours, let us kneel down! Let us give thanks to God! He has given me all my eight children: Let the house go; I am rich enough."

—From John Wesley's account of the Epworth fire on August 24, 1709[1]

DAY 1

Contemporary Words

This early experience of John Wesley has become part of the "Wesley legend." It has been told often and embellished in many ways. Was it an event that demonstrated that he was specially chosen by God? That is a possibility; however, I believe that through this story, we are reminded of a more fundamental truth. If that one person had decided to run off and get the ladder to save the young John, he would have never been more than the young John. The world would never have heard of John Wesley. The truth is that our lives are fragile. They are the only opportunity we have to live with passion and purpose...and, like Wesley, to make a mark upon the world.

WEEK TWO

My Words

How are you living TODAY—so as to make the gift of your life all that God has created it to be?

List some of the dreams you believe God might have for you.

Write about one step you could make today to move closer to one of those dreams.

COMING HOME

God's Words

They devoted themselves to the apostles' teaching and fellowship,
to the breaking of bread and to prayer.

—Acts 2:42 (NIV)

Wesley's Words

"The Birth of the Movement"

We may consider, First, the rise and progress of this work:...As to the rise of it. In the year 1725, a young student at Oxford was much affected by reading Kempis's "Christian Pattern," and Bishop Taylor's "Rules of Holy Living and Dying." He found an earnest desire to live according to those rules, and to flee from the wrath to come. He sought for some that would be his companions in the way, but could find none; so that, for several years, he was constrained to travel alone, having no man either to guide or to help him. But in the year 1729, he found one who had the same desire. They then endeavoured to help each other; and, in the close of the year, were joined by two more. They soon agreed to spend two or three hours together every Sunday evening. Afterwards they sat two evenings together, and, in a while, six evenings, in the week; spending that time in reading the Scriptures, and provoking one another to love and to good works.

—"On Laying the Foundation of a New Chapel," no. 132, 1.1

Contemporary Words

What was it that enabled Wesley to become such a leader? In the above passage, we can see some of the important pieces of his spiritual formation.

- He spent time in spiritual reading.

- He had an earnest desire to know God's will for his life and a willingness to live it even if it meant being alone.

- He actively sought companions to share the journey.

- He put himself in a situation wherein he was held accountable for his spiritual integrity by the scriptures and his companions.

DAY 2

My Words

How can this model of Wesley's early spiritual discipline shape your life as you seek a deeper connection with God?

<u>**Reading Spiritual Works**</u>

<u>**Seeking God's Will for My Life**</u>

<u>**Finding Spiritual Companions**</u>

<u>**Keeping Accountable**</u>

COMING HOME

God's Words

Then Barnabas went to Tarsus to look for Saul, and when he had found him, he brought him to Antioch. So it was that for an entire year they met with the church and taught a great many people, and it was in Antioch that the disciples were first called "Christians."

—Acts 11:25–26 (NRSV)

DAY 3

Wesley's Words

"From Whence the Name"

The regularity of their behaviour gave occasion to a young gentleman of the College to say, "I think we have got a new set of *Methodists*,"—alluding to a set of Physicians, who began to flourish at Rome about the time of Nero, and continued for several ages. The name was new and quaint; it clave to them immediately; and from that time, both those four young gentlemen, and all that had any religious connexion with them, were distinguished by the name of *Methodists*.

—"On Laying the Foundation of a New Chapel," no. 132, 1.2

Contemporary Words

In Antioch, the group under the teaching of Barnabas and Paul came to be known as Christians because they were followers of Christ. Another interpretation of the name is "little Christs." These people didn't choose the name. They didn't sit down and have a "let's name the group" session. People observed their life together and called them Christians.

The name Methodist was originally used as a derogatory term. People looked at the careful seriousness with which the young students practiced their faith and gave them the name "Methodists."

──── WEEK TWO ────

My Words

By what name would you be called as a result of observing the way you live out your spiritual life?

Write a description of some of the most important dimensions of your spiritual life.

By what name would you *like* to be called, and why?

COMING HOME

God's Words

Let no evil talk come out of your mouths, but only what is useful for building up, as there is need, so that your words may give grace to those who hear. And do not grieve the Holy Spirit of God, with which you were marked with a seal for the day of redemption. Put away from you all bitterness and wrath and anger and wrangling and slander, together with all malice, and be kind to one another, tenderhearted, forgiving one another, as God in Christ has forgiven you. Therefore be imitators of God, as beloved children, and live in love, as Christ loved us and gave himself up for us, a fragrant offering and sacrifice to God.

—Ephesians 4:29–5:2 (NRSV)

Wesley's Words

"Looking for Salvation by Following the Rules"

In the four or five years following, another and another were added to the number, till, in the year 1735, there were fourteen of them who constantly met together. Three of these were Tutors in their several Colleges; the rest, Bachelors of Arts or Under-graduates. They were all precisely of one judgment, as well as of one soul; all tenacious of order to the last degree, and observant, for conscience' sake, of every rule of the Church, and every statute both of the University and of their respective Colleges. They were all orthodox in every point; firmly believing not only the Three Creeds, but whatsoever they judged to be the doctrine of the Church of England, as contained in her Articles and Homilies. As to that practice of the Apostolic Church, (which continued till the time of Tertullian, at least in many Churches,) the having all things in common, they had no rule, nor any formed design concerning it; but it was so in effect, and it could not be otherwise; for none could want anything that another could spare. This was the infancy of the work. They had no conception of anything that would follow. Indeed, they took "no thought for the morrow," desiring only to live to-day.

—"On Laying the Foundation of a New Chapel," no. 132, 1.3

Contemporary Words

Passionate sincerity characterized these young "Methodists." With all their hearts, souls, and minds they pursued the fulfillment of the work of God in their lives. They drew on two sources for their pattern of behavior: the teachings and rules of the Church of England and their understanding of the practices of the early church. Both of these sources came from the well of church tradition. In the tradition of the Church, we find a record of the work of faithful generations who have gone before. It is a resource for us as we strive to live out our faith today.

DAY 4

—————————— WEEK TWO ——————————

My Words

What are some of the church traditions that are most important to you and why?

Traditions of the Church Year

Traditions in Worship

COMING HOME

God's Words

Remember the long way that the LORD your God has led you these forty years in the wilderness, in order to humble you, testing you to know what was in your heart, whether or not you would keep his commandments. He humbled you by letting you hunger, then by feeding you with manna, with which neither you nor your ancestors were acquainted, in order to make you understand that one does not live by bread alone, but by every word that comes from the mouth of the LORD.

—Deuteronomy 8:2–3 (NRSV)

Wesley's Words

"The Trip to Georgia (accompanied by the rules)"

Many imagined that little society would be dispersed, and Methodism (so called) come to an end, when, in October, 1735, my brother, Mr. Ingham, and I, were induced, by a strange chain of providences, to go over to the new colony in Georgia. Our design was to preach to the Indian nations bordering upon that province; but we were detained at Savannah and Frederica, by the importunity of the people, who, having no other Ministers, earnestly requested that we would not leave them. After a time, I desired the most serious of them to meet me once or twice a week at my house. Here were the rudiments of a Methodist society; but, notwithstanding this, both my brother and I were as vehemently attached to the Church as ever, and to every rubric of it; insomuch that I would never admit a Dissenter to the Lord's Supper, unless he would be re-baptized. Nay, when the Lutheran Minister of the Saltzburghers at Ebenezer, being at Savannah, desired to receive it, I told him, I did not dare to administer it to him, because I looked upon him as unbaptized; as I judged baptism by laymen to be invalid: And such I counted all that were not episcopally ordained.

—"On Laying the Foundation of a New Chapel," no. 132, 1.4

Contemporary Words

For all his piety and practice, powerful knowledge of the Bible, as well as adherence to Christian traditions, Wesley didn't do too well on his missionary journey to Georgia. He was so dedicated to the laws of the church and his own way of living out those laws (rules) that he was blinded to the needs and differences of those around him. His unwavering commitment to upholding the rules of the tradition became a stumbling block for him and his ministry.

DAY 5

WEEK TWO

My Words

Can you think of a time in which you have been so committed to "the way it has always been done before" that you might have missed something God was trying to tell you, or missed reaching someone God wanted to touch through you?

Write briefly about this experience.

NOTES

Endnotes

[1] Richard Heitzenriter, *The Elusive Mr. Wesley, Vol. 1* (Nashville: Abingdon Press, 1984), p. 36.

3 GOING DEEP

Discovering the Roots Of Authentic Spirituality

"Earth's crammed with Heaven,
and every common bush afire with God;
But only he who sees takes off his shoes -
The rest sit round it and pluck blackberries . . ."

—*"Aurora Leigh," Bk. 7, line 820*
Elizabeth Barrett Browning

GOING DEEP

Discovering the Roots of Authentic Spirituality

I knew I should have checked it sooner, but I had been so busy with getting ready for exams, then taking exams, then being glad that exams were over...Then, of course, I had to begin filling the 1966 VW bug full of laundry, and the drum set, and the albums (those were like big black plastic CDs that you couldn't play in the car) and the plants I couldn't leave in the dorm over the winter break. By the time I'd finished packing the car, it was probably too late to leave, but the dorms were closed, and I wanted to get home. "I can make it," I thought. "All I need is coffee." Five hundred miles through the middle of the night, already experiencing post-finals sleep deprivation syndrome—"No problem!" My reasoning was somewhat obscured by the pseudo invulnerability that comes from being nineteen. "I can do anything," I thought.

The moon was bright that night and stars filled the deep Southern sky. Now, here it was, well after midnight, somewhere along the highway in a very rural part of Mississippi (or was it Alabama?), and I noticed it. The needle in the only gauge, other than the speedometer, on the light blue metal dashboard was resting on the side of the gauge, just to the left of "E." Well, being the well-educated young man I was, I tapped the glass wondering why it was resting off to the side like that. Then a sudden realization of the problem swept over me: "It does that when there is no gas in the tank, which must mean . . ."

Just a few hours before, I had imagined I was invincible. I could take on anything. Now, I was alone in the middle of nowhere, in the middle of the night, in my little 1966 VW bug, just hoping I could make it to the next exit. Suddenly, the world seemed so much bigger and I felt so much smaller. The miles seemed longer than before. The fear of being stuck "out there" without any way to contact anyone increased (how used to cell phones I've become). I thought about the gas stations I'd passed on the way out of town. I remembered times when the tank had been full. I wondered what would happen if I poured the bottle of "Old Spice" aftershave in the gas tank. I tried to "will" the needle back to the right, but it was no use. First, a little cough, then a chug, small enough to almost believe that it was really nothing. Then a definite sputter. Then the sound of the engine stopped all together. The power driving the car, that I had somehow mistakenly assumed was my own power, ran out. For a while the car continued forward on its own. Rolling down the road in the moonlight in a landscape that had suddenly become strangely silent. I steered toward the shoulder. The gravel crunched beneath the tires until the car came to a stop. Then silence.

The experience of being forced to stop made it possible for me to see past the illusion of my own power to the need of a power beyond myself, and it helped me to realize that if you don't keep gas in the car on a regular basis, you will eventually encounter a situation wherein you need it, but there is nothing you can do about it on your own.

Up until that point, the evening had been filled with the sound and vibration that comes only from a '66 bug with a metal interior. It was a sound to which I had become accustomed. It was a sound that, along with maintaining my illusion of control and power, drowned out the songs of the fall leaves rustling in the trees and the cicadas singing in the recently stubbled cotton field.

I got out and walked around. I looked at the car. It still looked just like the thing that only a moment before had been propelling me forward through the night with power and purpose. Now it was empty. It had the form but not the power. It wasn't the car's fault. It got great mileage, but you still had to put gas in it. I'd been too busy to stop and look at the gas gauge.

Wesley's Concern

Wesley wrote, "I am not concerned that the people called Methodists should ever cease to exist, either in Europe or in America, but that they would continue to exist only as a dead sect, having the form of religion without the power." This week we will look at some of the reasons Wesley thought the church was not thriving as it could and see if those words speak to our own situation as individuals and as a church.

Spiritual Oat Bran or Mall Walking

The "means of grace" are not what give us a meaningful spiritual life. Life in and with God is a gift of grace. The "means of grace" are the practices that make it more able for us to allow God into our lives. Each day we will explore one of the "means of grace" during the reading and reflection time. Even if these activities seem uncomfortable at first, don't give up. Some of you may know what it is to restart or intensify an exercise program or a diet. It is less than comfortable, but if you stick with it, you will see great benefit.

This week, you have before you a "sampler" of some different types of spiritual exercises. Take your time and try to see which of these exercises might benefit you most.

GOING DEEP

God's Words

...holding to the outward form of godliness but denying its power. Avoid them!

—2 Timothy 3:5 (NRSV)

Wesley's Words

"What Makes a Christian?"

In these [places], every branch of Christianity is openly and largely declared; and thousands upon thousands continually hear and receive "the truth as it is in Jesus." Why is it then, that even in these parts Christianity has had so little effect? Why are the generality of the people, in all these places, Heathens still? no better than the Heathens of Africa or America, either in their tempers or in their lives? Now, how is this to be accounted for? I conceive, thus: It was a common saying among the Christians in the primitive Church, "The soul and the body make a man; the spirit and discipline make a Christian;" implying, that none could be real Christians, without the help of Christian discipline. But if this be so, is it any wonder that we find so few Christians; for where is Christian discipline? In what part of England (to go no farther) is Christian discipline added to Christian doctrine? Now, whatever doctrine is preached, where there is not discipline, it cannot have its full effect upon the hearers.

—"Causes of the Inefficacy of Christianity," no. 116, 7

DAY 1

Contemporary Words

In this sermon, Wesley is reflecting on the lack of effect that Christianity was having on the world of his day. There were plenty of churches and many people who gathered in them, but poverty, abuse, inhumane conditions, and the lack of education continued to be widespread. Christianity seemed common as a belief, but those who were believers seemed much the same as those who were not. There was much invested in the religion of the day. The church was powerful, the buildings were magnificent, yet the fact that there were Christians living in the world didn't seem to make much of a difference to the surrounding society. Why was that? The cause, says Wesley, is the lack of connection to the Spirit and Christian discipline. The Church without connection to the Spirit is like the '66 VW Bug without any gas—it has the form, but not the power. We can move toward reconnection by intentionally seeking a living and growing relationship through Christian discipline—regular participation in the "means of grace."

──────────────────── **WEEK THREE** ────────────────────

My Words

Practice being in the Presence of God. On this first day of reading and reflection this week, we will focus on drawing near to God and deepening the living relationship for which we were created. I invite you to take a little time and do something that will set your study or prayer place apart as a sacred place where you go to meet with God. Whether at home in a quiet place or on your lunch break in a busy office, you can do some simple things to remind yourself of the sacred nature of what you are doing.

Set up your space. Keep your Bible in the place where you will go to study and to pray. When you are finished with one day's reading, go ahead and open the Bible to the next day's reading and leave it there. Then it will be open and waiting for you, inviting you to return. You may want to keep a picture, or a cross, or an item in your space that helps you remember a time when you felt particularly close to God. One of the simplest and most effective things to do is to light a candle to remind yourself that Jesus said, "I am the light of the world." As you read, reflect, study and pray, while the candle is burning, you are reminded of the nearness of Christ.

Take a few moments to become quiet. Be open. Ask God to help you draw near. Wait... Take time to reflect on some of the experiences in your own life, big or small, looking for one wherein you can remember having sensed the presence of God.

Write what you remember of that experience.

Try to hold on to the experience of the nearness of God as you go from this place today and remember that presence even in the grocery-shopping, traffic-filled, stack-of-calls-waiting experience that is life.

GOING DEEP

God's Words

Then he said to them all, "If any want to become my followers, let them deny themselves and take up their cross daily and follow me."

—Luke 9:23 (NRSV)

Wesley's Words

"The Missing Ingredient"

But to return to the main question. Why has Christianity done so little good, even among us? among the Methodists,—among them that hear and receive the whole Christian doctrine, and that have Christian discipline added thereto, in the most essential parts of it? Plainly, because we have forgot, or at least not duly attended to, those solemn words of our Lord, "If any man will come after me, let him deny himself, and take up his cross daily, and follow me." It was the remark of a holy man, several years ago, "Never was there before a people in the Christian Church, who had so much of the power of God among them, with so little self-denial." Indeed the work of God does go on, and in a surprising manner, notwithstanding this capital defect; but it cannot go on in the same degree as it otherwise would; neither can the word of God have its full effect, unless the hearers of it "deny themselves, and take up their cross daily."

—"The Inefficacy of Christianity," no. 116, 13

DAY 2

Contemporary Words

Wesley's call to prayer is expected even in the midst of a hectic and demanding schedule:

"The reformers were probably almost as busy as we, yet their response to the daily grind was an inversion of our values and attitudes. And so Luther said, 'I'm so busy and burdened with these mounting responsibilities that unless I pray four hours a day I won't get all of my work done.' Later John Wesley wrote to the pastor of a small congregation who complained that Wesley was expecting too much by way of study and prayer: 'Oh, begin! Set some time each day for prayer and Scripture whether you like it or not. It is for your life! Else you will be a trifler all your days.'"

—Norman Shawchuck and Gustave Rath, *Benchmarks of Quality in the Church*, p. 15.[1]

—————————— WEEK THREE ——————————

My Words

Deepening the Experience of Formal Prayers

One of the complaints against written liturgy and formal, oft-repeated prayers is that they soon are memorized and become little more than a recitation of words without the heart, soul, or mind ever getting into the experience. As one who loves to spend time at the monastery I know the value of the printed liturgy and the presence of God in the prepared word. I do agree, however, that if we are not careful, we can fall into the habit of simply reading without being engaged by the words. One simple exercise to keep the words of ancient prayers and liturgies fresh is paraphrasing, or putting the writing into your own words. Today we will try it with the familiar passage, the Lord's Prayer.

Our Father, who art in Heaven, Hallowed be thy name.

Thy Kingdom come, Thy will be done, on Earth as it is in Heaven.

Give us this day our daily bread, and forgive us our trespasses as we forgive those who trespass against us.

Lead us not into temptation, but deliver us from evil, for thine is the Kingdom and the power and the glory, forever. Amen.

GOING DEEP

God's Words

Command those who are rich in this present world not to be arrogant nor to put their hope in wealth, which is so uncertain, but to put their hope in God, who richly provides us with everything for our enjoyment. Command them to do good, to be rich in good deeds, and to be generous and willing to share. In this way they will lay up treasure for themselves as a firm foundation for the coming age, so that they may take hold of the life that is truly life.

—1 Timothy 6:17–19 (NIV)

Wesley's Words

"Learning the Secret of Stewardship"

Why is not the spiritual health of the people called Methodists recovered?... O why do not we, that have all possible helps, "walk as Christ also walked?" Hath he not left us an example that we might tread in his steps? But do we regard either his example or precept? To instance only in one point: Who regards those solemn words, "Lay not up for yourselves treasures upon earth?" Of the three rules which are laid down on this head, in the sermon on "The Mammon of Unrighteousness," you may find many that observe the First rule, namely, "Gain all you can." You may find a few that observe the Second, "Save all you can:" But how many have you found that observe the Third rule, "Give all you can?"

—"Causes of the Inefficacy of Christianity," no. 116, 8

Contemporary Words

Why is the church not as alive as it could be and as alive as we would want it to be if we had invited Jesus to lunch? The reason is the lack of surrender. We tend to try to hold on to control. We want to be in control of the way things happen in church, in our financial lives, and even in our relationships. I find it much easier to say, "Not what you want, Lord, but what I want. Oh, and by the way, this is the way I'd like it." In his sermon, "On the Use of Money," Wesley said, "Earn all you can, save all you can, and give all you can." He knew that the practice of hard work, and careful saving coupled with a willingness to give freely and trust in God's provision aids in the development of compassionate and committed disciples, along with a church that has the resources to make a difference in the world. Many are good at earning, and some at saving, but missing is a passionate life of giving that demonstrates our hope in God and not in the wealth God enabled us to earn.

WEEK THREE

My Words

Ask and Reflect. Does my giving demonstrate:

- **My trust in God's providence rather than my wealth?**

- **My passionate commitment to the work of Christ through the church?**

- **My concern for the poor and the broken?**

- **What kind of gift would be sacrificial for me and honoring to God? What is something I could do specifically?**

GOING DEEP

God's Words

Woe to you, scribes and Pharisees, hypocrites! For you tithe mint, dill, and cummin, and have neglected the weightier matters of the law: justice and mercy and faith. It is these you ought to have practiced without neglecting the others. You blind guides! You strain out a gnat but swallow a camel!

Woe to you, scribes and Pharisees, hypocrites! For you clean the outside of the cup and of the plate, but inside they are full of greed and self-indulgence. You blind Pharisee! First clean the inside of the cup, so that the outside also may become clean.

—Matthew 23:23–26 (NRSV)

Wesley's Words

"There is No Power in the Means Themselves"

Secondly, before you use any means, let it be deeply impressed on your soul,—there is no *power* in this. It is, in itself, a poor, dead, empty thing: Separate from God, it is a dry leaf, it is a shadow. Neither is there any *merit* in my using this; nothing intrinsically pleasing to God; nothing whereby I deserve any favor at his hands, no, not a drop of water to cool my tongue. But, because God bids, therefore I do; because he directs me to wait in this way, therefore here I wait for his free mercy whereof cometh my salvation.

—"Means of Grace," no. 16, V. 4

Contemporary Words

One of the biggest misconceptions about spiritual exercises and religious rituals is that there is something intrinsically valuable about them, that if we just say prayers, or take communion, we somehow will be privileged by God. The other misconception is that liturgical practices and spiritual disciplines stand in the way of real and direct experience of God. Wesley had to struggle with arguments surrounding these misconceptions. On one side were the people deeply embedded in the traditional practices of the church who were afraid of the new movement toward spiritual renewal, with an emphasis on an experience of God. On the other side were those who were so committed to the immediate experience of God that they rejected any formal prayers or ritual as obstructions to an authentic spiritual life. Wesley, as he did in so many things, was able to see what was valuable in both sides. While he knew the value of a living relationship with a living God, he also knew the benefit of the practice of particular spiritual exercises. He is clear that these exercises are not the goal of the religious life, but are merely means to the end, which is a transformed and transforming life of discipleship.

────────────── **WEEK THREE** ──────────────

My Words

** **Materials needed for this session:** a Bible, a cup (empty or filled with water or grape juice), some bread (a slice will do), and a picture or other representation of Jesus.*

Holy Communion: I once had a conversation with a rabbi who had visited a church during a communion service. His fresh perspective helped me see two things. First, he reflected on what a powerful symbolic activity it was. It engaged the five senses of touch, taste, sight, sound, and smell. It carried with it a conceptual dimension and a spiritual expression. "What a beautiful and powerful thing, to be able to come to the altar together and take God inside of you." The other reflection was less flattering. After he had just expressed deep reverence for the sacrament and the depth of its meaning, he said, "It seems that most people are going up there as if it is just another task to do, like picking something up at the grocery store. If I had a sacrament like that, I would want to savor it and experience it to the fullest." It took an encounter with someone outside the church to help me understand how potentially powerful our own sacrament is.

Read Mark 14:22–25. Look at your picture or other representation of Jesus and think about the actual person there in that room talking to the disciples. Try to imagine what it looked like. **What were the sights and sounds? What were the smells? What were the feelings and emotions?**

Hold the bread. Imagine the hands of Jesus holding bread.

What does he mean when he says, "This is my body?"

How is he "broken for you?" What does that mean for you personally?

Hold the cup. **How is he "poured out for you?"**

Next time you participate in Holy Communion, allow these memories and images to surround you.

GOING DEEP

God's Words

"Now therefore revere the LORD, and serve him in sincerity and in faithfulness; put away the gods that your ancestors served beyond the River and in Egypt, and serve the LORD. Now if you are unwilling to serve the LORD, choose this day whom you will serve, whether the gods your ancestors served in the region beyond the River or the gods of the Amorites in whose land you are living; but as for me and my household, we will serve the LORD."

—Joshua 24:14–15 (NRSV)

Wesley's Words

"Becoming Like God"

I would earnestly advise you, Fourthly: "Keep in the very path wherein you now tread. Be true to your principles." Never rest again in the dead formality of religion. Pursue with your might inward and outward holiness; a steady imitation of Him you worship; a still increasing resemblance of his imitable perfections,—his justice, mercy, and truth.

—"Advice to the People Called Methodists"

Contemporary Words

Just before taking them across the river into the Promised Land, Joshua held up a choice before the people who would be making the journey. It wasn't a choice about what to believe. It was a choice about whether or not they would put away anything that competed for their total allegiance to God.

In his "Advice to the People Called Methodists," Wesley gives the same type of instruction. The life of a believer is not to be just the outer practices of attending a service or joining a particular congregation. The life of the believer is to be a life that seeks holiness, both inward and outward. It is to be a life that strives to grow closer to God in character and in relationship.

──────────── **WEEK THREE** ────────────

My Words

Think back over the week and some of the times of reflection you have had.

How are you becoming more aware of the deep places and the growing edges of your spiritual life?

Take a moment and be quiet in the presence of God. Listen. Wait. Just breathe and quiet your mind.

Write a letter to God about how you see your relationship, and where you want to grow closer. List two or three specific things that you can put into practice in the coming week that will help develop that process.

Dear God,

When you are finished writing, close your eyes and imagine offering the letter to God and staying there while God reads it.

How does God respond?

NOTES

Endnotes

[1] Norman Shawchuck and Gustave Rath, *Benchmarks of Quality in the Church* (Nashville: Abingdon Press, 1994) p. 15.

4 OUTSIDE THE GATES

Getting to Know the Cultures in Our Context

And so Jesus also suffered outside the city gate to make the people holy through his own blood.

—Hebrews 13:12 (NIV)

OUTSIDE THE GATES

Getting to Know the Cultures in Our Context

We heard him as we passed through the square before we went to dinner, and now as we made our way back toward the subway (or the "Tube," as it is called in London), we saw that he had not given up. In fact, the crowd had grown from a handful of onlookers to several dozen, all listening to the man who was singing for tips with an acoustic guitar and a battery-powered amp. The neon lights for the theatres and the "McDonald's" sign seemed somewhat out of place mounted on buildings that are several centuries old. The square was filled with people. All of them seemed to be headed somewhere. They moved at varying degrees of speed and with varying levels of purposeful intensity. Some of them looked as if they were headed to or from work, some to dinner or a show. A woman with face furrowed in anger walked quickly through the crowd while a slightly embarrassed and apologetic looking man hurried to catch up. Sightseeing parents with children tired from a day of exploration shuffled and tugged their way towards rest. It was a crossroads. It was a gathering place. It was a square filled with people from many different walks of life, different cultures, and even from different parts of the world.

The sounds, too, seemed to clutter the evening with their diversity—the roar of the double-decker buses moving an endless flood of people through Piccadilly Circus a couple of blocks over, the impatient blare of the horns of taxi drivers rushing to drop their human cargo while looking towards the next fare, the whistles of the police, the sirens of the emergency vehicles, the homeless man's request for spare change and the rattle of the pennies in his cup, the raucous voice of the drunk who was trying to get someone to dance with him, people speaking, or yelling, or laughing in a dozen different languages, all merging together into the constant cry of the ceaseless motion which is the city.

Then I heard something that changed the purpose of my listening. The sound I heard called me as a participant in the newly emerging melody of the familiar, a simple sound, the chords and the light picking of a song I remembered from high school. Something stirred within me, and I wanted to join with the guitar-playing leader of our spontaneous congregation. I couldn't help it. Suddenly, I found myself singing along like a youth at a bonfire. I was singing James Taylor's "You've Got a Friend." As I sang, I noticed that my wife was singing, too. With our arms around each other's waists, we sang. The music took center stage in the midst of the perpetual motion all around.

"You just call out my name,
And you know wherever I am,

I'll come running, to see you again...
...and I'll be there, yes I will.
You've got a friend."[1]

We sang as if that was what we had come there that evening to do, and as I looked around I saw that we weren't the only ones who had been carried into this moment of spontaneous song. The dozens who had paused to listen all seemed to be singing as well, and many more had stopped their frantic motion and had gathered around the shared melody. As I looked around the circle at the faces of those singing, I was moved even more deeply, for even though we were all singing in English, those whose voices were lifted were from India, Japan, the Middle East, different countries in Europe, America, and who knows how many other places. The singers were old and young; even the homeless man ceased the rattling of the cup and sang. For a moment the sound of the city had disappeared and there, in the middle of London, late at night, thousands of miles away from home, in the midst of a crowd of strangers from all over the world, I caught a glimpse of what it must have been like on the day of Pentecost.

Why was it that "You've Got a Friend" struck such a chord in the hearts of all of those people from all over the world? I think it was because the song touched a common human need or longing...the need to know that someone cares enough to come to us when we are hurting, or afraid, or alone. Wesley was called out beyond the walls of the to touch people who would have resonated with the feelings in that song. They were lost and alone. They were working as hard as they could, but couldn't make enough to get out of poverty. The children grew up in a world in which they saw parents with no education struggling day after day just to keep bread on the table. They had no opportunities for education, so they soon entered the poverty cycle. Many drank the cheap gin to escape the hopelessness of the situation and to dull the pain of deprivation.

It was to these people that the words of Wesley's preaching came and brought a message of real hope. The words came to remind them that there was someone who cared for them, not just for their souls in an afterlife that seemed, at times, too far away, but for them in the here and now. This was a message that was brought to the people outside the gates of the church in the 1700s.

What did it take?

At Pentecost, the noise of a people brought together for a celebration was transformed into the song of a people who were celebrating because they had been brought together. In the midst of diversity, a message emerged that spoke to the need in the heart of all who had gathered.

During the Wesleyan revival, the song swelled again:

"O for a thousand tongues to sing my great Redeemer's praise,
The glories of my God and King, the triumphs of His grace!"

What are the barriers to our moving outside the gates, or even opening the doors and welcoming those who are outside into our midst? What are the possibilities for ministry that await us?

And so Jesus also suffered outside the city gate to make the people holy through his own blood. Let us, then, go to him outside the camp, bearing the disgrace he bore. For here we do not have an enduring city, but we are looking for the city that is to come.

Through Jesus, therefore, let us continually offer to God a sacrifice of praise—the fruit of lips that confess his name. And do not forget to do good and to share with others, for with such sacrifices God is pleased.

Hebrews 13:12–16

OUTSIDE THE GATES

God's Words

Dear friends, since God so loved us, we also ought to love one another.

—1 John 4:11 (NIV)

Wesley's Words

"If we can't think alike, can't we still love alike?"

3. All men approve of this; but do all men practice it? Daily experience shows the contrary. Where are even the Christians who "love one another as He hath given us commandment?" How many hinderances lie in the way! The two grand, general hinderances are, First, that they cannot all think alike; and, in consequence of this, Secondly, they cannot all walk alike; but in several smaller points their practice must differ in proportion to the difference of their sentiments.

4. But although a difference in opinions or modes of worship may prevent an entire external union; yet need it prevent our union in affection? Though we cannot think alike, may we not love alike? May we not be of one heart, though we are not of one opinion? Without all doubt, we may. Herein all the children of God may unite, notwithstanding these smaller differences. These remaining as they are, they may forward one another in love and in good works.

—"The Catholic Spirit," no. 39, 3–4

DAY 1

Contemporary Words

Sometimes I drive through a section of the city in which I live that has obvious evidence of deep poverty. It is an area that is considered to be dangerous because of the frequency of violent crime. I reached over and pushed the auto lock button on the door as I sat at the traffic light. Then I looked up at the billboard above me. It was one of those plain black billboards with simple white writing. It said, "That love one another thing—I meant it. God"

I found myself in one of those rough and honest moments of self-examination in which I came up short of what I thought I believed. Maybe I do believe that I ought to love one another, just as God loves me. Maybe the problem is not so much in the right belief as it is in the right practice, or lack thereof. I wonder how my life would be different if I actually lived the command to love rather than just agreeing with it in my mind...?

—————————— WEEK FOUR——————————

My Words

Can you remember a time in which you or someone very close to you was broken, far from God, in the midst of doing something wrong, or was otherwise difficult to love?

Try to think through some of the details of that situation and write them down. (*These will not be for sharing.*)

What was the nature of the hurt?

How was this person far from God?

At the deepest point in this person's brokenness and pain, how was he/she seen and loved by God?

How are we to relate to those who are broken or far from God?

Think of one person you need to love more fully.

What one thing can I do to love this person in a concrete way?

OUTSIDE THE GATES

God's Words

When he left there, he met Jehonadab son of Rechab coming to meet him; he greeted him, and said to him, "Is your heart as true to mine as mine is to yours?" Jehonadab answered, "It is." Jehu said, "If it is, give me your hand."

—2 Kings 10:15 (NRSV)

Wesley's Words

"The Need to be Right"

It is certain, so long as we know but *in part*, that all men will not see all things alike. It is an unavoidable consequence of the present weakness and shortness of human understanding, that several men will be of several minds in religion as well as in common life....Farther: Although every man necessarily believes that every particular opinion which he holds is true; (for to believe any opinion is not true, is the same thing as not to hold it;) yet can no man be assured that all his own opinions, taken together, are true. Nay, every thinking man is assured they are not; seeing . . "To be ignorant of many things, and to mistake in some, is the necessary condition of humanity." This, therefore, he is sensible, is his own case. He knows, in the general, that he himself is mistaken; although in what particulars he mistakes, he does not, perhaps he cannot, know.

I say, perhaps he cannot know; for who can tell how far invincible ignorance may extend? or (that comes to the same thing) invincible prejudice?—which is often so fixed in tender minds, that it is afterwards impossible to tear up what has taken so deep a root...

Every wise man, therefore, will allow others the same liberty of thinking which he desires they should allow him; and will no more insist on their embracing his opinions, than he would have them to insist on his embracing theirs. He bears with those who differ from him, and only asks him with whom he desires to unite in love that single question, "Is thy heart right, as my heart is with thy heart?"

—"Catholic Spirit," no. 39, 3–6

Contemporary Words

One of the main attitudes constraining churches from a healthy and growing focus on the mission field outside our gates is the ever-present need to "be right." We want to feel that what we believe is God's absolute and complete truth. Because of this belief, it is natural for us to see those who hold thoughts or beliefs that are different from ours as wrong. This attitude affects us on two fronts: first, it can allow us to miss our opportunity for mission if we remain clustered with others who think, act, and believe exactly as we do. Secondly, if this attitude of self-righteousness takes root inside the church, causing argument and divisiveness to characterize our community, it can cause us to miss the opportunity for effective witness as well.

WEEK FOUR

My Words

Think of a time when a disagreement in thought or belief has kept you from being open to reaching out to a person who was different from you.

Write a description of the situation.

Think of a time when you have seen a divisiveness within the church that prevents members from being a positive witness to those outside the church.

Record your thoughts and feelings about this situation.

Reread and underline the third paragraph in the "Wesley's Words" section on page 64.
What kind of difference would it make to my church if I were willing to "bear with those who differ," and offer my hand? Record your thoughts below.

OUTSIDE THE GATES

God's Words

What good is it, my brothers, if a man claims to have faith but has no deeds? Can such faith save him? Suppose a brother or sister is without clothes and daily food. If one of you says to him, "Go, I wish you well; keep warm and well fed," but does nothing about his physical needs, what good is it? In the same way, faith by itself, if it is not accompanied by action, is dead.

—James 2:14–17 (NIV)

Wesley's Words

"Can True Love be Passive?"

Is thy heart right toward thy neighbour? Dost thou love, as thyself, all mankind without exception? "If you love those only that love you, what thank have ye?" Do you "love your enemies?" Is your soul full of good-will, of tender affection, toward them? Do you love even the enemies of God, the unthankful and unholy? Do your bowels yearn over them? Could you "wish yourself" temporally "accursed" for their sake? And do you show this by "blessing them that curse you, and praying for those that despitefully use you and persecute you?"

Do you show your love by your works? While you have time, as you have opportunity, do you in fact "do good to all men," neighbours or strangers, friends or enemies, good or bad? Do you do them all the good you can; endeavouring to supply all their wants; assisting them both in body and soul, to the uttermost of your power?—If thou art thus minded, may every Christian say, yea, if thou art but sincerely desirous of it, and following on till thou attain, then "thy heart is right, as my heart is with thy heart."

—"Catholic Spirit," no. 39, 17–18

Contemporary Words

In James, we hear about the worthlessness of wishing hurting people well without trying to touch them at the point of their need. I believe that the same is true of love. If we simply say, we love as Jesus loved, but keep that love inside our churches or inside our minds, then we are missing the point. I once took a course in scuba diving. As part of the test for certification, we had to go to the bottom of the deepest part of the pool, remove our tanks, disassemble them, and breathe directly off the tank. I saw some people try to inhale the tiny stream of bubbles while under water and begin to cough. Those people shot to the surface with a purpose and passion I had not witnessed in them before. Their urge to preserve self became their central focus. In that light, let us ask, what does it mean to love your neighbor as yourself? I believe it has something to do with urgency and a willingness to act.

———————————— WEEK FOUR ————————————

My Words

Take a few moments to reflect upon the community surrounding your church.

Who lives "outside the gates" and who is different from you?

Ask Jesus to help you see them as he sees them. Spend time in prayer.

Ask Jesus to help you love them as he loves them. Spend time in prayer.

What actions can you think of that would appropriately express Christian love to these persons? List what you can do.

OUTSIDE THE GATES

God's Words

But God demonstrates his own love for us in this: While we were still sinners, Christ died for us.

—Romans 5:8 (NIV)

Wesley's Words

"Accepting each other as Christ has accepted us"

I do not mean, "Be of my opinion." You need not: I do not expect or desire it. Neither do I mean, "I will be of your opinion." I cannot: It does not depend on my choice: I can no more think, than I can see or hear, as I will. Keep you your opinion; I mine; and that as steadily as ever. You need not even endeavour to come over to me, or bring me over to you. I do not desire you to dispute those points, or to hear or speak one word concerning them. Let all opinions alone on one side and the other: Only "give me thine hand."

—"Catholic Spirit," no. 39, II.1

DAY 4

Contemporary Words

God's love for us is not based on our behavior or belief. God's love for us is unconditional. This kind of love is the model of love for people in God's community. The diversity of the early Methodist people was much like the diversity of the people who made up the early church. There were people of different religious traditions and differing schools of thought. There were people from various educational levels. There were people from every point on the socio-economic spectrum. In the midst of this complex mixture of people groups, it was very important for Wesley to help individuals develop an attitude of acceptance of people unlike themselves. It was this spirit of acceptance that provided the foundation for the new community in the midst of diversity.

WEEK FOUR

My Words

List some "opinions" that separate Christians.

Look again at the previous page. Read carefully and underline the sentence in the "Wesley's Words" section, beginning with "Keep you your opinion; I mine..."

Do you have a relationship with someone inside or outside the church in which you could practice this advice?

How would you begin?

———————— WEEK FOUR ————————

OUTSIDE THE GATES

God's Words

Love is patient; love is kind; love is not envious or boastful or arrogant or rude. It does not insist on its own way; it is not irritable or resentful; it does not rejoice in wrongdoing, but rejoices in truth. It bears all things, believes all things, hopes all things, endures all things.

—1 Corinthians 13:4–7 (NRSV)

Wesley's Words

"Seeing With Eyes of Hope and Love"

Love me (but in a higher degree than thou dost the bulk of mankind) with the love that is *longsuffering and kind*; that is patient; if I am ignorant or out of the way, bearing and not increasing my burden; and is tender, soft, and compassionate still;—that *envieth not*, if at any time it please God to prosper me in his work even more than thee. Love me with the love that *is not provoked*, either at my follies or infirmities; or even at my acting (if it should sometimes so appear to thee) not according to the will of God. Love me so as to *think no evil* of me; to put away all jealousy and evil-surmising. Love me with the love that *covereth all things*; that never reveals either my faults or infirmities;—that *believeth all things*; is always willing to think the best, to put the fairest construction on all my words and actions;—that *hopeth all things*; either that the thing related was never done; or not done with such circumstances as are related; or, at least, that it was done with a good intention, or in a sudden stress of temptation. And hope to the end, that whatever is amiss, will, by the grace of God, be corrected; and whatever is wanting, supplied, through the riches of his mercy in Christ Jesus.

—"Catholic Spirit," no. 39, II. 4

Contemporary Words

It is so easy to look out from behind the walls of the church, or our homes, or our established communities and see those who are different as a threat to "life as we know it." Differences in thought, opinion, behavior, or belief often make us uncomfortable and quick to judge or distance ourselves from "them." Yet, it is to those who were different that Jesus went. It was with "them" that he spent his time. It was to them that he offered unconditional love, and it was for them that he eventually gave his life. In the same way, Wesley felt called and responded to those who were different, broken, and outside the context of the life of the church in that day. He tried to see people as Christ saw them, through the eyes of love and hope.

—————— WEEK FOUR——————

My Words

Have you ever been in a situation wherein you were called on to love some-one you were not naturally drawn to love? Describe the situation.

What did you find difficult?

What were the emotions you can remember?

How did you do?

What do you think it means that "Love bears all things, believes all things, hopes all things and endures all things?"

Endnotes

[1] Carole King and James Taylor, *Mudslide Slim and Blue Horizon*, Warner Brothers Records, W22561, 1971.

5 CLEAR EXPECTATIONS

We Each Play a Part

For we are God's servants, working together; you are God's field, God's building.

—1 Corinthians 3:9 (NRSV)

CLEAR EXPECTATIONS

We Each Play a Part

The news is not good. His cholesterol numbers are off the chart. His blood pressure indicators are soaring way beyond the safe level. "The doctor told me I am a walking time-bomb" are the words that come from the mouth of my twenty-six-year-old best friend. "Is there anything I can do to help?" I ask. "Well, yes, as a matter of fact there is. You can get up every morning and ride bikes with me for an hour before class." (This is one of those moments like at dinner when you see the last piece of chicken on the plate—you know you want it, but, because it is the right thing to do, you ask, "Anyone want this last piece?" and someone says "yes"...) I mean, after all, it is Denver, Colorado, in the winter. It is frigid. There is snow. Class starts at 8:00 A.M., which means getting out of the warmth of the bed before the sun is up, bundling up in layers, unimagined when I lived in Atlanta. It means facing wind chill that would double its chilly bite as we plunged through the icy air, wheeling our way toward Washington Park to see geese sitting on the frozen lake. It is one of those moments wherein it seems easier and more enjoyable to pretend that we have no connection with those close to us, or that we have no responsibility to help those with whom we have been given the journey of life. It would seem easier to stay in bed, but there on the bike, daily, as the sun breaks over the Denver skyline and splashes upon the face of the Rocky Mountains, two bundled seminary students, dressed like sleeping bags, learn the power of accountability.

Most of us have good intentions. Most of us are also extremely capable of being distracted from fulfilling those intentions. There were many mornings there in Denver, I am sure, that if I had not had my friend waiting for me out at the bike rack, I would have been able to rationalize some good reason to stay in bed just a little longer. There were many mornings, I am sure, that if my friend had not known that I would be knocking on his door, waking his wife and him if he left me standing alone at the bike rack, that he would have been able to conjure in his mind some good reason to stay in bed just a little longer. Yet, as with mountain climbers who, while roped to another climber, ascend to heights they would not attempt alone, we daily met and rode, lost weight and got healthy, and in the process watched, up close, the winter turning to spring. We saw the beauty of dew covered tulips at sunrise pushing their heads through melting snow as those same geese balanced upon the last pieces of ice which had solidly covered the lake a month before. We raced each other. We discussed classes. We discussed theology and faith. Instead of an extra hour under the blanket, we shared experiences of the unfolding beauty of the creative hand of God and in the midst of it, shared questions, thoughts, fears, doubts, hopes, and dreams. Not a bad trade.

Excitement, dreams, decisions, and intention all have value, yet without accountability, they are apt never to get past our ability to convince ourselves that it would be easier to stay in bed just a little longer. Accountability is a powerful force. It was a powerful force in the development of the Methodist movement.

George Whitfield, a contemporary of John Wesley, was one of the most dynamic and powerful preachers of the day. He was known for his ability to draw a crowd and leave them "spell-bound." His preaching in Bristol stirred the fire that became a large-scale revival. Whitfield preached for conversion and was very effective. Thousands of people responded to the call to "turn to Christ." He drew the crowds, held their attention, captured their imaginations and called for conversion. The crowds responded. Thousands of people were called to new life. Thousands of people responded. Thousands experienced conversion.

If the purpose is simply to get people to make a decision for Christ then "revival preaching" would be enough. If, however, the purpose is to bring people into a relationship with Christ that transforms their lives and the world around them in a lasting way, then something is needed to sustain the activity and commitment that otherwise would fade as soon as the immediate experience of the conversion has faded. Something more than "revival" preaching is needed. Something more than individual conversion is required. This is where John Wesley's understanding of accountability, discipleship formation, and leadership development, coupled with organizational genius, emerged as an answer to the need.

In the context of this new ministry, Wesley remembered words spoken to him when he was younger that had shaped his understanding of the journey of discipleship. "Sir, you wish to serve God and go to heaven. Remember that you cannot serve Him alone. You must therefore find companions or make them. The Bible knows nothing of solitary religion."[1] This understanding was what motivated his leadership of the Holy Club at Oxford. He knew that the fire of conversion was soon extinguished if it was left to burn alone, but when combined with others who were like-minded, the chances for success were much greater.

This week, our readings will focus on the development of the process of discipleship formation and leadership development that Wesley developed around the idea of accountability in the midst of ministry.

CLEAR EXPECTATIONS

God's Words

But you are a chosen people, a royal priesthood, a holy nation, a people belonging to God, that you may declare the praises of him who called you out of darkness into his wonderful light. Once you were not a people, but now you are the people of God; once you had not received mercy, but now you have received mercy.

—1 Peter 2:9–10 (NIV)

Wesley's Words

"Royal Priesthood, Holy Nation"

He is raising up those of every age and degree, young men and maidens, old men and children, to be "a chosen generation, a royal priesthood, a holy nation, a peculiar people; to show forth His praise, who hath called them out of darkness into his marvelous light." And we have no reason to doubt, but he will continue so to do, till the great promise is fulfilled; till "the earth is filled with the knowledge of the glory of the Lord, as the waters cover the sea; till all Israel is saved, and the fullness of the Gentiles is come in."

"Wisdom of God's Counsels," no. 68, 23

DAY 1

Contemporary Words

Although Wesley had grown up in a minister's family and was very familiar with the rules of the church, he developed a profound sense of the importance of the ministry of the laity. At first, he was hesitant about allowing those who were not ordained by the church to be ones who proclaimed the Gospel, but his mother encouraged him not to react to the idea without first looking to see if the preaching bore fruit. As Wesley witnessed the growth of the movement and the increasing demands and opportunities for preaching and ministry, he spent more time and effort developing leaders from among the converts. Wesley's itinerant preachers were often laymen and sometimes even laywomen. The Wesleyan revival was a powerful example of the ministry in the hands of the laity with the clergy providing leadership, organization and the sacraments. The work of the church was in the hands of the people and the people were the priests.

This idea of the priesthood of all believers provides us with an important dimension of identity that so often is missing in church. As part of God's royal priesthood, we are gifted to serve and given opportunities for service as well as responsibility to serve as bearers of God's activity in the world.

——————————— **WEEK FIVE** ———————————

My Words

What does it mean for you to be a member of a congregation? What does it mean for you to be a follower of Christ? How does it inform your identity? Does it give you a particular purpose or direction?

Read the following paragraph from The United Methodist Book of Discipline[2] *and answer the following questions in light of this paragraph.*

¶ 219. All members of Christ's universal church are called to share in the ministry which is committed to the whole church of Jesus Christ. Therefore, each member of The United Methodist Church is to be a servant of Christ on mission in the local and worldwide community. This servanthood is performed in family life, daily work, recreation and social activities, responsible citizenship, the stewardship of property and accumulated resources, the issues of corporate life, and all attitudes toward other persons. Participation in disciplined groups is an expected part of personal mission involvement. Each member is called upon to be a witness for Christ in the world, a light and leaven in society, and a reconciler in a culture of conflict. Each member is to identify with the agony and suffering of the world and to radiate and exemplify the Christ of hope. The standards of attitude and conduct set forth in the Social Principles (Part IV) shall be considered as an essential resource for guiding each member of the Church in being a servant of Christ on mission.

What is the role of a layperson?

What does it mean for me to be a member of a royal priesthood?

CLEAR EXPECTATIONS

God's Words

Enlarge the site of your tent, and let the curtains of your habitations be stretched out; do not hold back; lengthen your cords and strengthen your stakes. For you will spread out to the right and to the left, and your descendants will possess the nations and will settle the desolate towns.

—Isaiah 54:2–3 (NRSV)

Wesley's Words

"Building to House the Ministry"

We took possession of a piece of ground, near St. James's church-yard, in the Horse Fair, where it was designed to build a room, large enough to contain both the societies of Nicholas and Baldwin-Street, and such of their acquaintance as might desire to be present with them, at such times as the Scripture was expounded. And on Saturday, 12, the first stone was laid, with the voice of praise and thanksgiving.

—*Journal,* May 9, 1739

DAY 2

Contemporary Words

Even though, as a "Fellow" of Lincoln College at Oxford, Wesley supposedly had the approval and the authority of the church to preach in any pulpit in the land, he found himself barred from churches all across the country. People saw him as a radical who took the religion thing too seriously. There were even several instances of mobs attacking him while he was preaching or stoning houses where his meetings were held. In the face of this controversy Wesley didn't lose hope or focus but forged ahead and took steps to ensure that the ministry that was happening would not be derailed. He didn't build a church building in the traditional sense of the term, but he did build a building that was well designed to house the work of a movement.

The New Room in Bristol was at once a meeting house for the new converts, a mission center for ministry with the poor, and a training house and residence for the much-needed new generation of leadership. It may look rather simple to us today, but it was creatively designed, efficient, and as "high-tech" as any structure of its era. It was designed to house a different model of training than the type Wesley experienced at Oxford, but it was a model of education and training that kept those who were responding to the call close to the ministry field, in service, and meeting needs as they learned to lead. The New Room was a building designed to accomplish the purpose of the church, instead of a building that, as so often is the case, shapes the ministry of the people who gather there.

—————————————— **WEEK FIVE** ——————————————

My Words

Reflect upon these questions and write your responses below each section.

What characteristics do you look for in leaders?

What kind of characteristics do you look for in a layperson in church leadership? How do you identify and develop leaders in your church?

What is needed for someone to be a good pastor?

When was the last time someone entered into pastoral ministry from your church?

CLEAR EXPECTATIONS

God's Words

Bear with one another and, if anyone has a complaint against another, forgive each other; just as the Lord has forgiven you, so you also must forgive. Above all, clothe yourselves with love, which binds everything together in perfect harmony. And let the peace of Christ rule in your hearts, to which indeed you were called in the one body. And be thankful. Let the word of Christ dwell in you richly; teach and admonish one another in all wisdom; and with gratitude in your hearts sing psalms, hymns, and spiritual songs to God. And whatever you do, in word or deed, do everything in the name of the Lord Jesus, giving thanks to God the Father through him.

—Colossians 3:13–17 (NRSV)

Wesley's Words

"Gathering for Accountable Discipleship"

Such a society is no other than "a company of men having the form and seeking the power of godliness, united in order to pray together, to receive the word of exhortation, and to watch over one another in love, that they may help each other to work out their salvation."

That it may the more easily be discerned, whether they are indeed working out their own salvation, each society is divided into smaller companies, called classes, according to their respective places of abode. There are about twelve persons in every class; one of whom is styled *the Leader*. It is his business, (1.) To see each person in his class once a week at least, in order to inquire how their souls prosper; to advise, reprove, comfort, or exhort, as occasion may require; to receive what they are willing to give toward the relief of the poor. (2.) To meet the Minister and the Stewards of the society once a week; in order to inform the Minister of any that are sick, or of any that walk disorderly, and will not be reproved; to pay to the Stewards what they have received of their several classes in the week preceding; and to show their account of what each person has contributed.

—"The Nature, Design, and General Rules of the United Societies," 2–3

Contemporary Words

The class meeting was designed for the care and accountability of the people. It was where people had their close, face-to-face relationships and were able to ask questions and have discussions that enabled their faith to grow. It was the group that provided Christian care for one another during illness or the loss of a job. The class leader was one of their own who had been given training in the care of the group. Together, they could strive to live out new life in Christ. Together they had a better chance at succeeding than they did alone.

DAY 3

—————————————— **WEEK FIVE** ——————————————

My Words

The class meetings provided people with an opportunity to discuss the struggles that all people face, yet most hide. It was this ability to discuss that gave them the strength and encouragement to attempt to live more faithfully. The questions used during the meetings seem very direct, but they were effective. Spend some time with the questions below and respond in writing to each of them. If there is something that comes to mind that you don't want to write about, ask yourself "why?" and consider what it would be like if you had a person or group with whom you could openly discuss your struggles.

1. What known sins have you committed since our last meeting?

2. What temptations have you met with?

3. How were you delivered?

4. What have you thought, said, or done, of which you doubt whether it be sin or not?

CLEAR EXPECTATIONS

God's Words

Do not be deceived; God is not mocked, for you reap whatever you sow. If you sow to your own flesh, you will reap corruption from the flesh; but if you sow to the Spirit, you will reap eternal life from the Spirit. So let us not grow weary in doing what is right, for we will reap at harvest time, if we do not give up. So then, whenever we have an opportunity, let us work for the good of all, and especially for those of the family of faith.

—Galatians 6:7–10 (NRSV)

Wesley's Words

"Salt and Light"

There is one only condition previously required in those who desire admission into these societies,—a desire "to flee from the wrath to come, to be saved from their sins:" But, wherever this is really fixed in the soul, it will be shown by its fruits. It is therefore expected of all who continue therein, that they should continue to evidence their desire of salvation. First, by doing no harm, by avoiding evil in every kind; especially that which is most generally practiced ....Secondly, by doing good, by being, in every kind, merciful after their power; as they have opportunity, doing good of every possible sort, and as far as is possible, to all men...

—"The Nature, Design, and General Rules of the United Societies," 4–5

DAY 4

Contemporary Words

It is very important to provide clear expectations for those who are choosing to be followers of Christ. The leaders of the class meetings are serious about keeping people accountable to growth in the Christian life. Providing clear expectations is not an overly zealous way to impose a particular moral standard; it is a set of boundaries in which one could not only live in healthy community and spiritual growth but also make a difference in the lives of others. Followers are to be those who not only avoid evil but also do all the good they could find to do. What a difference in perspective and possibility emerges from persons who are struggling for survival in a "look-out-for-number-one world," and through Christ, find themselves striving for holiness with a group of supportive people!

—— WEEK FIVE ——

My Words

Consider that you are hearing the following instructions as part of the expectations of membership in your church. **What, specifically, would they mean to your life? What do you find meaningful? What do you find problematic? Write your responses below each section.**

DIRECTIONS GIVEN TO THE BAND-SOCIETIES DECEMBER 25, 1744

You are supposed to have the faith that "overcometh the world."
To you, therefore, it is not grievous,—

I. Carefully to abstain from doing evil; in particular,—

1. Neither to buy nor sell anything at all on the Lord's day.

2. To taste no spirituous liquor, no dram of any kind, unless prescribed by a Physician.

3. To be at a word both in buying and selling.

4. To pawn nothing, no, not to save life.

5. Not to mention the fault of any behind his back, and to stop those short that do.

6. To wear no needless ornaments, such as rings, earrings, necklaces, lace, ruffles.

7. To use no needless self-indulgence, such as taking snuff or tobacco, unless prescribed by a Physician.

II. Zealously to maintain good works; in particular,—

1. To give alms of such things as you possess, and that to the uttermost of your power.

2. To reprove all that sin in your sight, and that in love and meekness of wisdom.

3. To be patterns of diligence and frugality, of self-denial, and taking up the cross daily.

CLEAR EXPECTATIONS

God's Words

Let us hold fast to the confession of our hope without wavering, for he who has promised is faithful. And let us consider how to provoke one another to love and good deeds, not neglecting to meet together, as is the habit of some, but encouraging one another, and all the more as you see the Day approaching.

—Hebrews 10:23–25 (NRSV)

Wesley's Words

"Clear Expectations"

It is expected of all who desire to continue in these societies, that they should continue to evidence their desire of salvation, Thirdly, by attending upon all the ordinances of God. Such are, the public worship of God; the ministry of the word, either read or expounded; the supper of the Lord; family and private prayer; searching the Scriptures; and fasting, or abstinence.

These are the General Rules of our societies; all which we are taught of God to observe, even in his written word, the only rule, and the sufficient rule, both of our faith and practice. And all these, we know, his Spirit writes on every truly awakened heart. If there be any among us who observe them not, who habitually break any of them, let it be made known unto them who watch over that soul as they that must give an account. We will admonish him of the error of his ways; we will bear with him for a season: But then if he repent not, he hath no more place among us. We have delivered our own souls.

—"The Nature, Design, Rules of the United Societies," 6–7

DAY 5

Contemporary Words

Membership was meaningful in the societies because it made a difference and it had clear expectations. People were motivated to work through the process of individual transformation and to enter into a ministry activity that would make a difference in the world around them because these expectations were clearly defined and there was accountability. Low expectations produce low commitment and yield poor results. High expectations produce high commitment and yield good results. What does this idea of clear expectations say to us as a church today?

———— Week Five ————

My Words

If someone were to ask you the following questions about your church how would you respond? Write your answers in the space provided below.

What must I do to become a member?

What are the expectations of me as a member?

What happens if I don't fulfill the expectations?

NOTES

Endnotes

[1] Percy Livingstone Parker, ed. *The Journal of John Wesley* (Chicago: Moody Press, 1951), p.20.

[2] *The United Methodist Book of Discipline 2000* (Nashville: The United Methodist Publishing House, 2000), pp.131–132.

6 THE EMERGING CHURCH

Uncovering Our Ancient Future

"My people have committed two sins:
They have forsaken me,
the spring of living water,
and have dug their own cisterns,
broken cisterns that cannot hold water."

—*Jeremiah 2:13 (NIV)*

THE EMERGING CHURCH

Uncovering Our Ancient Future

The sunlight filtered into the room in soft warm stripes sliced by the Venetian blinds hanging in the window and fell across the faces of the people, some kneeling, some standing with hands open, some praying, some singing. It was a moment of prayer and consecration. It was a moment of recognition. Surrounded by towering pines and the foothills of the ancient Appalachian Mountains in a valley named "resting place," or *Sumatanga* in the language of the Native Americans who originally inhabited the area, we had come to learn and grow as faithful church leaders, as ministers both clergy and lay, in this time of great change and challenge. We had gathered for a closing service of communion and consecration.

The Bishop had come to bless and commission those who were completing their training at the Academy for Congregational Development. His sermon was designed to challenge the participants, to commission them for their work, and to send them out with a calling to be the church today, whatever that may look like...to focus on making disciples and not on maintaining institutions. He told of the powerful effect the church had had on his life and on the world around him as he was growing up. He told the difficult truth about the state in which many churches find themselves today—people getting older and fewer in numbers, people wondering why there were no young people coming and worried about the future of the church. He spoke directly to these leaders and, with passion, called them to lead in ways that would reach out beyond the walls of the church and do the work of God in their neighborhoods, cities, and towns. I liked his talk. It resonated with me at a deep level.

After the sermon, the participants came forward for a time of blessing and commissioning and during that time, they participated in a renewal of their baptismal vows. They felt again the touch of the water, and remembered that with that water, the symbol of Baptism, came not only a new life characterized by grace and forgiveness, but also a new life characterized by the entrance into the priesthood of all believers. In the touch of that water, they were reminded that they were part of the Body of Christ, and given gifts for service and the building up of the body. The Bishop had brought a bowl to hold the water for the baptismal renewal. It was a special bowl that had been given to him as a gift when he was in Africa. He had used it for this purpose on many occasions. Beautiful, hand-carved wood sat on the table, between the candles holding the water that told the story of redemption and new life.

As my wife played the piano and led the music for this closing service and the participants filed forward, I watched prayerfully. It was beautiful to see. They were taking it seriously. They were soaking it in. They were alive and ready to be touched and sent out for God. After talking about the challenge, after praying over the water as a symbol of God's Holy Spirit and the power to renew, he called people forward to renew their covenant.

Then it happened. Something that could not be planned happened that spoke to me louder than words. I was sitting on the side. As a leader for the weekend retreat, I was helping with the music and was waiting for the other participants to go forward. I noticed a drip of water coming off of the table. I watched the drips increase. Something had spilled. I looked more closely. I don't know how, but during the prayer for the water and for the renewal and reformation of the church, that beautiful old wooden bowl that had held so much memory and had held so much meaning had split and the water was pouring out on the floor. At first I thought, "how terrible...," but then I saw the gift.

What a powerful symbol!

> *...that beautiful old wooden bowl that had held so much memory and had held so much meaning had split and the water was pouring out on the floor.*

Sometimes the structures we have designed as instruments to share the life-giving message of God split, no matter how beautiful they are, no matter how useful and meaningful they have been, no matter how much we love them. Sometimes they split. They cease to function as they once had, like the church in Wesley's day. At that point we have choices. One choice is to be so attached to the bowl for nostalgic or sentimental or loyalty reasons that we hang on to the bowl as the water drains away. Another choice is to try to repair, or get a new bowl so we can do what is really important—the faithful sharing of that powerful truth that has come to us alive from the past which is our responsibility to deliver, with all of its life, to children and grandchildren yet to come. "I will pour out my Spirit," says the Lord. What is the state of our bowl?

During this final week, we will be looking at readings from the scripture and readings from Wesley's writings that emerge out of times of rebuilding when the bowls had cracked. Through the scriptures we will look at the return of those who had been exiled from the Promised Land and their rebuilding of the Temple. We will also look at the concluding challenge in Wesley's sermon that was delivered to the people who gathered on the day they laid the foundation for the City Road Chapel in London. It is a challenge that was given to those who had either witnessed or had participated in one of the greatest renewal movements ever experienced in the history of Christianity. In both of these situations, the people were called to faithfulness. They were called to difficult faithfulness and commitment in an important time of change.

THE EMERGING CHURCH

God's Words

This is what the LORD says: "Stand at the crossroads and look; ask for the ancient paths, ask where the good way is, and walk in it, and you will find rest for your souls.

—Jeremiah 6:16 (NIV)

Contemporary Words

In the words of the prophet Jeremiah, spoken to the people of Israel just before the exile, there was heard a call to return to the "ancient paths." The same message was spoken by John Wesley. Wesley was a defender of what was called "Primitive Christianity." He believed that the truth of Christianity, as well as the model for faithfulness in the future, was to be found in the past—in the model of church found in the book of Acts. The renewal in the days of Wesley was brought about by a return to the "ancient paths." Today, there are many churches that, once again, are returning to this model and looking to the past for a roadmap to the future. I believe the emerging effective church in the twenty-first century will be a church with an ancient future.

DAY 1

Wesley's Words

How is Your Experience?

All of the "Wesley's Words" sections in this chapter are taken from the concluding challenge in the sermon written on the day the foundation was laid for the new chapel headquarters in London. The readings do not correspond directly with the Scripture and the commentary; however, I have placed the words here as a fitting challenge for us as we consider how we will live in this time of change and choice.

Brethren, I presume the greater part of you also are members of the Church of England. So, at least, you are called; but you are not so indeed, unless you are witnesses of the religion above described. And are you really such? Judge not one another; but every man look into his own bosom. How stands the matter in your own breast? Examine your conscience before God. Are you a happy partaker of this scriptural, this truly primitive, religion? Are you a witness of the religion of love? Are you a lover of God and all mankind?

—"On Laying the Foundation of the New Chapel," no. 132, 17

—————————— **WEEK SIX** ——————————

My Words

John considered himself to be a defender of primitive Christianity as recorded in the book of Acts. Read the passage below and underline the practices of the early church that illustrate for you the heart of Christianity.

> They devoted themselves to the apostles' teaching and to the fellowship, to the breaking of bread and to prayer. Everyone was filled with awe, and many wonders and miraculous signs were done by the apostles. All the believers were together and had everything in common. Selling their possessions and goods, they gave to anyone as he had need. Every day they continued to meet together in the temple courts. They broke bread in their homes and ate together with glad and sincere hearts, praising God and enjoying the favor of all the people. And the Lord added to their number daily those who were being saved.

—Acts 2:42–47 (NIV)

Journal your responses to the following questions:

Which elements in the above passage are present in your religious life?

Which elements are missing?

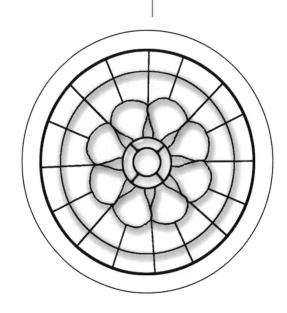

THE EMERGING CHURCH

God's Words

This is what Cyrus king of Persia says:

"The LORD, the God of heaven, has given me all the kingdoms of the earth and he has appointed me to build a temple for him at Jerusalem in Judah. Anyone of his people among you—may his God be with him, and let him go up to Jerusalem in Judah and build the temple of the LORD, the God of Israel, the God who is in Jerusalem. And the people of any place where survivors may now be living are to provide him with silver and gold, with goods and livestock, and with freewill offerings for the temple of God in Jerusalem."

—Ezra 1:2–4 (NIV)

Contemporary Words

In despair, in exile, suddenly there is a ray of hope. "We can go home?!"

Some of the Israelites knew where home was and what it was like. They had been alive when they were forced to leave. They are elated to be going home, but know deep down that it will be difficult because it would not be the same as when they had left it.

Others had only heard stories about "home." They had grown up knowing nothing but life in exile. Their place of exile was home, and they were not sure that going back to their ancestral "home" would be worth the effort.

It was to these people that the call to return home came. The people of God were called to pick up what they had been doing for seventy years, to make the long journey back to the ancient place, and to begin the work of rebuilding what had once stood to the glory of God.

Wesley's Words

"How is Your Witness?"

Does your heart glow with gratitude to the Giver of every good and perfect gift, the Father of the spirits of all flesh, who giveth you life, and breath, and all things; who hath given you his Son, his only Son, that you "might not perish, but have everlasting life?" Is your soul warm with benevolence to all mankind? Do you long to have all men virtuous and happy? And does the constant tenor of your life and conversation bear witness of this?

—"On Laying the Foundation of the New Chapel," no. 132, 17

DAY 2

— WEEK SIX —

My Words

The world the Israelites encountered in exile was a very different world from the Promised Land. The experience of the people who remembered the Promised Land was very different from the experience of those who had only known exile. I believe there are some similarities between those groups and the different generations that populate our churches today.

In *Resident Aliens*,[1] Will Willimon and Stanley Hauerwas point to a time, very different from today, when I believe the church felt at home and in its "Promised Land:"

> You see, our parents had never worried about whether we would grow up Christian. The church was the only show in town. On Sundays, the town closed down. One could not even buy a gallon of gas. There was a traffic jam on Sunday mornings at 9:45, when all went to their respective Sunday schools. By overlooking much that was wrong in the world—it was a racially segregated world, remember—people saw a world that looked good and right...Church, home, and state formed a national consortium that worked together to instill "Christian values." People grew up Christian simply by being born in places like Greenville, South Carolina, or Pleasant Grove, Texas.
>
> —*Resident Aliens*, p. 16

When you were growing up, was the church in the Promised Land, or was it in exile? Explain your answer.

Write about your memories of what it was like to be a child going to church.

What is different today for children and youth as they come to church?

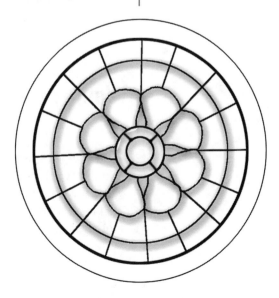

THE EMERGING CHURCH

God's Words

When the seventh month came and the Israelites had settled in their towns, the people assembled as one man in Jerusalem. Then Jeshua son of Jozadak and his fellow priests and Zerubbabel son of Shealtiel and his associates began to build the altar of the God of Israel to sacrifice burnt offerings on it, in accordance with what is written in the Law of Moses the man of God. Despite their fear of the peoples around them, they built the altar on its foundation and sacrificed burnt offerings on it to the LORD, both the morning and evening sacrifices. Then in accordance with what is written, they celebrated the Feast of Tabernacles with the required number of burnt offerings prescribed for each day. After that, they presented the regular burnt offerings, the New Moon sacrifices and the sacrifices for all the appointed sacred feasts of the LORD, as well as those brought as freewill offerings to the LORD. On the first day of the seventh month they began to offer burnt offerings to the LORD, though the foundation of the LORD'S temple had not yet been laid.

—Ezra 3:1–6 (NIV)

DAY 3

Contemporary Words

Those who responded to the call to rebuild God's temple knew how important their task was. They knew that it would take more than their own efforts. They knew that the venture would be successful only if it was powerfully connected to God and emerged from a responsiveness to the direction and will of God. Before they started rebuilding, before they laid the foundation, they built an altar and made their offerings to God. Wesley also knew that religion was nothing if it was only words, beliefs, and lifeless ritual. He believed that what was needed was a faith which was rooted in a living relationship with God and which was lived out in every dimension of daily life.

Wesley's Words

"How is Your Love?"

Do you "love, not in word" only, "but in deed and in truth?" Do you persevere in the "work of faith, and the labour of love?" Do you "walk in love, as Christ also loved us, and gave himself for us?" Do you, as you have time, "do good unto all men;" and in as high a degree as you are able? *Whosoever thus* "doeth the will of my Father which is in heaven, the same is my brother, and sister, and mother."

—"On Laying the Foundation of the New Chapel," no. 132, 17

— WEEK SIX —

My Words

Before launching into the project of rebuilding, the people of God spent time in prayer and in the offering of sacrifices. Ask God to show you how your church might be better equipped or aligned to reach out to younger generations.

Spend ten minutes in silence listening, then write your thoughts in the space below.

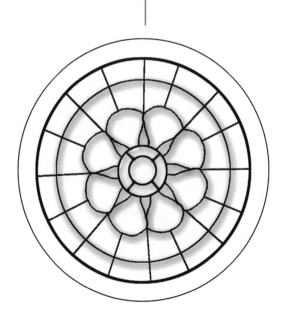

THE EMERGING CHURCH

God's Words

When the builders laid the foundation of the temple of the LORD, the priests in their vestments and with trumpets, and the Levites (the sons of Asaph) with cymbals, took their places to praise the LORD, as prescribed by David king of Israel. With praise and thanksgiving they sang to the LORD:

"He is good;

his love to Israel endures forever."

—Ezra 3:10–11 (NIV)

Contemporary Words

What a day that must have been. Everyone was gathered together to witness something that had started with a call from God and a response of a faithful people. It took faith. It took prayer. It took commitment. But most of all, it took being willing to step out and move in the direction to which God was calling, and go where God already was. Armed with that kind of faith and the knowledge that "God's love endures forever," they were able to reconnect with God for the renewal of God's people.

DAY 4

Wesley's Words

"How is Your Longing?"

Whosoever thou art, whose heart is herein as my heart, give me thine hand! Come, and let us magnify the Lord together, and labour to promote his kingdom upon earth! Let us join hearts and hands in this blessed work, in striving to bring glory to God in the highest, by establishing peace and good will among men, to the uttermost of our power! First. Let our hearts be joined herein; let us unite our wishes and prayers; let our whole soul pant after a general revival of pure religion and undefiled, the restoration of the image of God, pure love, in every child of man!

—"On Laying the Foundation of the New Chapel," no. 132, 17

—————————— **WEEK SIX** ——————————

My Words

Think of someone from a previous generation who greatly affected your life or faith.

Write that person's name and something about him or her that affected you.

Think about someone in a younger generation who is important to you. Think about what can you do for that person, or for others in that age group, that would positively affect their lives and help them develop a strong sense of the goodness and enduring love of God.

Write down the name of the person and list some things you might be able to do to positively affect this person's life. (*List as many individuals as you like.*)

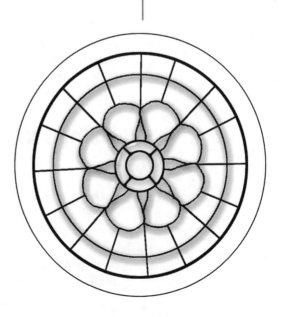

THE EMERGING CHURCH

God's Words

And all the people gave a great shout of praise to the LORD, because the foundation of the house of the LORD was laid. But many of the older priests and Levites and family heads, who had seen the former temple, wept aloud when they saw the foundation of this temple being laid, while many others shouted for joy. No one could distinguish the sound of the shouts of joy from the sound of weeping, because the people made so much noise. And the sound was heard far away.

—Ezra 3:11–13 (NIV)

Contemporary Words

Imagine that sound. Imagine the sound of thousands of people—trumpets sounding, cymbals crashing—and a sound rising from the crowd that was somewhat confusing.

Some of the people who were old enough to remember the Temple, upon seeing the foundation of the new one built on the rubble of the old, were overcome with sorrow. They broke down and filled the air with weeping and wailing. They knew that a new temple had to be built in order to transfer faith from generation to generation, but it was difficult to see the old one pass away.

The others, who had been born in captivity, who had never seen the old temple, and who, for the first time, were seeing the work of God unfold in the world through their efforts and sacrifices, were overflowing with joy. Their shouts filled the air with cheers and with laughter. Imagine that sound.

Cymbals and trumpets, weeping and cheering—so loud that you could hear them far away. What a day that must have been. It was a day of struggle and fulfillment, a day of pain and joy. Different generations worked, prayed, and sacrificed together; and from different memories and perspectives combined their efforts to insure that the love of God would be passed on to generations yet to come.

Wesley's Words

"How is Your Action?"

Then let us endeavour to promote, in our several stations, this scriptural, primitive religion; let us, with all diligence, diffuse the religion of love among all we have any intercourse with; let us provoke all men, not to enmity and contention, but to love and to good works; always remembering those deep words, (God engrave them on all our hearts!) "God is love; and he that dwelleth in love dwelleth in God, and God in him!"

—"On Laying the Foundation of the New Chapel," no. 132, 17

DAY 5

— WEEK SIX —

My Words

Close your eyes and imagine that day recorded in the book of Ezra on which the foundation had been laid and there was great celebration and sadness. What made people happy? What made them sad?

With this in mind, read the following questions and journal your responses.

As you look at some of the challenges facing our church in the present day:

1) What are some things that make you feel like the ones who had been part of the old Temple and hated to see it pass away?

2) What are some things that cause you to be happy and excited as you look at the new things that God is calling churches to do in order to reach out to new generations?

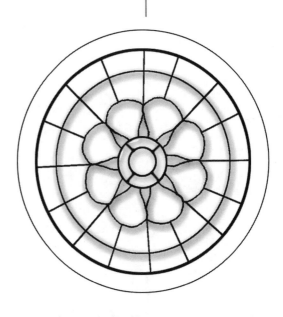

Notes

Endnotes

[1] William H. Willimon and Stanley Hauerwas, *Resident Aliens: Life in the Christian Colony* (Nashville: Abingdon Press, 1990).

7 LET'S ROLL

Living Out the Vision In the Local Church

"Let's roll."

　　　　—Todd Beamer, 9/11/01 before leading the passengers to wrestle control from the terrorist hijackers.

"A journey of ten thousand miles begins with a single step."

　　　　　　　　　　　　　　　　　—Anonymous proverb

LET'S ROLL

Living Out the Vision In Our Congregation

The final section is to be completed during the closing session after watching the video. These pages contain an invitation to pray for your church and its ministry as well as an invitation to open your heart and mind to dream God's dreams for you. After spending time in prayer and reflection, you will have an opportunity to share ideas with the group.

The next steps in the process are up to you. This journey can have been a fun learning experience, or it can be the beginning of renewal for you, your congregation, and maybe even the church as a whole. In the following pages, you will find some suggestions on how to use what you have learned to help others share the vision for a dynamic renewal of the church as in the days of John Wesley. Please take some time to read the following section, to pray, and to share your ideas with one another.

Pray

Either as a group or individually, commit to pray for your church and its ministry. Pray and listen to God for direction and energy.

Write words or phrases that come to mind as you ask God about the future of your church. (*Remember that God, through prevenient grace, is already there; our job is to go where God already is.*)

How is God speaking to me at this time about my life of faith and the life of my church?

Who are those outside the gates of our church with whom we may be being called into ministry?

If there is nothing standing in the way, what would God be calling me and/or our congregation to do?

Where do I see the ministry of my congregation in five, ten, fifteen, or twenty years?

What are my "God-sized dreams" for the life and ministry of our congregation?

My Next Steps

Write down three things that you can agree to do right away to help your congregation move into God's future.

ReConnecting
A Wesleyan Guide for the Renewal of Our Congregation

Rob Weber

If you or your congregation are longing for something that will help create a climate of excitement, energy, purpose, passion, and connection with the changing world and our changeless God, then get ready to begin this journey of reconnection!

This is what people who have experienced *ReConnecting* had to say:

"Wow! So that's who we are. I'm glad to be part of a church that can help change my life and make a difference in the world." *Shane, age 31*

"*ReConnecting* became the "buzz-word" at our church. People became excited about the future of our ministry. It was just what we needed." *Linda, age 46*

"I've gained a new perspective on ministry beyond the walls of the church and I can't wait to get involved." *John, age 47*

"Now I understand why some churches are developing new styles of worship in order to reach new generations of people." *Bob, age 72*

ReConnecting is a seven-week or seven-session experience designed to help your congregation reconnect with some of the major themes and principles in the ministry of John Wesley. However, this experience does not simply provide a lesson in Wesleyan history or theology. These themes and principles are applicable to all churches and all generations, and their recovery is meant to transform and re-energize the journey of discipleship on both the personal and corporate level. *ReConnecting* may be customized and used in a variety of settings—as an adult Lenten study, as a renewal program, or as a study of Wesleyan heritage.

Note to Group Leaders:
You will need to purchase the Leader's Guide with DVD, ISBN 0-687-02234-7 to prepare for the sessions. This is the Participant's Guide and does NOT include a DVD.

Rob Weber is Senior Pastor and Founder of Grace Community United Methodist Church in Shreveport, Louisiana. Grace Community is a teaching church, with seeker-sensitive ministries that serve over 1200 in worship attendance each week (www.gracehappens.org). Rob Weber is in demand as a speaker for church leadership events throughout the world, including England, Korea, and the USA.

Abingdon Press
Cover Design: Cindy Caldwell
Tree Photo: © Don Tremain/GettyImages, Inc.
Hand with Seedling: © SuperStock Inc.

ISBN 0-687-06535-6

9 780687 065356   90000

Participant's Guide & Daily Journal

WHEN I STOOD ON THE

72nd hole of the 2001 PGA Championship at Atlanta Athletic Club, I was faced with the most important decision of my career. I was one stroke ahead of Phil Mickelson and needed a par to earn my first major championship—or, at the very least, to clinch a spot in a playoff should Phil make birdie. But I had a dilemma. I had driven the ball into the first cut of rough on the 490-yard par-4 18th hole and was facing a tough second shot into a green guarded by water front and left.

It was then that I recalled the hours of work that I had put into my short game with my teacher, Rob Akins. I was so confident in my short game that I knew if I laid up, I could get up and down for that all-important par.

And that's exactly what happened. Instead of trying to play the hero and pull off a miraculous 5-wood shot to the green, I placed the burden on my wedge and my putter to take me to my first major. After laying up, I stuck my wedge shot 12 feet from the hole, then watched as Phil left his birdie putt short. As I stood over that 12-footer, the long hours I had spent on practice greens from Louisiana to California seemed like the best time I had ever spent. Halfway there, I knew the putt was pure.

After that story, I don't think I need to tell you the level of importance I place on the short game. Rob and his co-author, Charlie King, understand exactly what I am talking about.

Rob and I grew up together in Shreveport, Louisiana, where we played junior golf against one another. It was then, after I had so thoroughly whipped him, that he decided his real future was in teaching, not playing.

Every student—myself included—who has ever benefited from Rob's teaching will tell you that that was the best decision he ever made. After you read this book. I have no doubt that you will agree.

> **Rob and Charlie have created a simple plan for short game improvement that will take your game to a new level.**

Rob and I began our student-teacher relationship in 1994, when I was a young, aspiring pro with a lot to learn. In 1996, Rob became my primary, full-time swing coach, and the results speak for themselves. Over these last 13-plus years, I have been fortunate enough to play consistent, championship-level golf, and I owe much of my success to Rob's solid teaching principles, his infectious passion for the game and his unmatched motivational skills.

Now, you can benefit from those very same things. The drills, games and information that Rob and I use in our short game practice sessions are now available to you in this innovative book.

Rob and Charlie have created a simple plan for short game improvement that will take your game to a new level. Their "Red Zone" drills, their motivational techniques and their simple, direct approach to teaching will have you playing your best golf from 100 yards and in.

Taking a lesson with either Rob or Charlie can require months to schedule, but you can start learning from them today. By following the simple program they lay out in this book, you can start posting the best scores of your life.

You may not win a major, but I can guarantee that Rob and Charlie will help you enjoy the game more than you ever have.

– David Toms

1

THE ATHLON RED ZONE

FIRST THINGS FIRST–

you're probably asking yourself what the Red Zone has to do with golf. That term is most familiar to football fans, who know the Red Zone as that space on the football field from the 20-yard line to the end zone. It's where games are won and lost.

Fans live and die with the Red Zone proficiency of their favorite teams. How many times have you heard a comment like this: "We've moved it all day long between the 20s, but we can't score when we get close." It's absolutely critical for teams to take advantage of their Red Zone opportunities—scoring a touchdown, or at worst, a field goal—if they want to win games. (If you're not a football fan, just work with us on this.)

Guess what? In a very real sense, golf is no different. We've simply borrowed a term from football and applied it to that space on a golf course—100 yards from the green and in—where, just like in football, you can make the biggest impact on your score.

You want to be better at golf—otherwise, you wouldn't have bought this book. In our combined four-plus decades of teaching golf, we have never met a person who didn't want to get better. Our daily lessons with golfers of all skill levels tell us that golfers are searching for that magic cure, for that secret formula that results in better golf.

And among all the golfers we've encountered, we have yet to meet one who doesn't know how important the short game is. Yet we very rarely see golfers working on the short game as hard as the full swing. Apparently, cranking out a 275-yard drive is more fun than hitting a wedge shot stiff, executing a deft chip shot or holing a 10-foot putt.

But we contend that those wedges, chips and putts are more important to your score than a booming long game.

Here's our guarantee: If you work on your short game—on your "Red Zone" skills—you'll see your scores improve.

Think of golf's Red Zone this way. Hole the ball out or get up and down in two shots, and you have scored a touchdown. Get up and down in three shots and you have kicked a field goal.

Taking four or more to get down from 100 yards and in? Well, that's like missing a field goal, or worse, throwing an interception and having it returned for a touchdown.

One more football analogy: You've certainly heard it said that defense wins championships. In golf, think of the full swing as your flashy offense and the short game as your championship-winning defense.

It's that important.

We have heard all the objections: "I'll start caring about the short game as soon as you can get me on or near the green in regulation. I don't care about getting up and down for a 10."

Those objections are understandable. The full swing and the long game are vitally important. But we don't think players fully appreciate the impact that Red Zone improvement can have on their enjoyment of the game.

> "Think of the full swing as your flashy offense and the short game as your championship-winning defense."

We had a common desire to do something about this problem. So we did, and we're thrilled with the results. We believe we've created a program that golf has never seen, one that combines motivation to improve your short game with easy-to-follow steps for getting there.

We want you to take the Athlon Red Zone Challenge that's presented in the pages that follow. By taking our simple test, giving yourself a short game handicap and following our 12-week program, you'll watch your scores plummet.

As you proceed with this program, we also invite you to go to **www.athlonsports.com** for more detailed short game instruction from Rob, Charlie and Athlon's elite team of instructors.

And here's a bonus: The habits you will learn in this book for pitching and chipping will help the full swing!

The ultimate Red Zone moment:
Larry Mize chips in to beat Greg Norman
at the 1987 Masters.

If you came to us on the lesson tee, we would look you in the eye and say, "We challenge you to see what your potential is. No excuses." We're doing the same thing with this book.

Unlike many golf teaching program—some of which you may be intimately familiar with—we're not going to give you a few tips or gimmicks and send you on your way. We are going to arm you with the tools you absolutely need to succeed. Many instruction books tell you "what," but you also need to know "how," "how much," "when" and "how often." Our program answers all of those questions, giving you the complete short game instruction book that you deserve.

We are finally giving you what has been available in every other sport for years: a clear series of steps to follow to become better. In basketball, you learn to dribble, pass, shoot, play defense, etc., through a series of progressive drills that makes playing basketball second nature. In learning to type, you follow a pattern that insures your improvement through learning the keys, then measures your progress with timed tests. Learning to swim involves a clear series of steps: floating, leg kick, arm motion and breathing.

What if we tried to skip a few steps in learning to type or swim? Would we be able to get a few tips from Typing Digest to make up for those missing habits? We all know the answer. Our habits will determine how good we are at typing. Does it take hours of prac-tice per day to become a proficient typist? No. It takes consistent-ly doing the right things for a reasonable period of time (a 3.5-month semester is pretty common for those learning in school).

We are asking you to commit 12 weeks to our program and fol-low all the all the steps we outline here. As with any other serious pursuit, you will develop habits that will become second nature to you.

You have the potential to be better than you are right now. What is a 12-week commitment when you can gain a lifetime of better golf? We just ask that you trust us. We've done the work and performed the research, and we can recall hundreds and even thousands of students who have enjoyed dramatic improvement.

Here's a quick example: When I first saw Michael he had just shot 127 in a tournament. It was a shock to his system. He knew he wasn't a great player, but he thought his game would hold up better in competition than that. Over the next several weeks he learned the principles you are going to learn in this book. He set up a practice routine similar to the platinum time plan you will learn about, and within 12 weeks his short game had improved dramatically. Within 14 months he had broken 80, and he now regularly shoots in the mid-70s.

This could be you.

"We challenge you to see what your potential is. No excuses."

"

I had teachers whose
philosophies changed from
week to week, and a couple who
simply did not care. It was a disgrace. Their examples taught
me what not to do.
And I can make that
knowledge work for you.
— Charlie King

"

I GOT A LATE START IN GOLF.

My Golf Story

— Charlie King

Tour players don't normally take up the game at age 19. But after five years of learning golf on my own, I had a low single-digit handicap, and a chance elective class I took in college led to the far-fetched idea of becoming a PGA Tour player (far-fetched according to my family and friends, anyway). That elective was called "Special Topics in Business Management." I needed one more elective hour and I heard it was an easy A. I was two quarters away from graduation and still didn't know what I wanted to do with my life. Our textbooks were *Think and Grow Rich* by Napolean Hill and *How to Win Friends and Influence People* by Dale Carnegie. One day, midway through the quarter, the professor came in and said something that changed my life. He asked: "If you could do anything you wanted to do and there was no limit on what you could do, what would you choose to do?" I had never thought about it that way. My passion for golf was to the point that I could be first on the tee at 7:00 am Saturday and Sunday, but couldn't quite get myself out of bed for my 9:00 am classes during the week. I had attended the 1987 Masters and witnessed one of the greatest shots in golf history, the chip-in by Larry Mize on the 11th hole to beat Greg Norman in a playoff, so it seemed logical to me to answer my professor's question with: "I would win the Masters." Inspired, I went to my two-bedroom apartment and got out a notebook. I wrote down my goal to win the Masters at the top and wrote the steps it would take from A to Z. I pursued my dream as hard as I could for four years. Then, at age 28, having had very limited success, I decided it was time to move on. But, needless to say, there had been benefits to chasing my dream, even if they weren't immediately evident. I had worked with several teachers in addition to becoming one myself. My first teacher "methodized" me with a one-size fits all approach that was ridiculous, to say the least. I had teachers whose philosophies changed from week to week, and a couple who simply did not care. It was a disgrace. Their examples taught me what not to do. And I can make that knowledge work for you. I have no idea if I could have made it on Tour, but **I deserved a chance to reach my potential. And so do you.** You deserve an approach that makes sense. In the pages that follow, we'll lay out that approach, clearly and concisely, and if you follow our system for 12 weeks you will see tremendous improvement in your game in as little as 5 minutes a day. Guaranteed. Enjoy the process, and start playing the golf you have only dreamed of playing.

2

THE
RED ZONE
SKILLS TEST

WHY DON'T PEOPLE

practice their short game when they know how important it is? We think there are lots of reasons, and we understand them.

- The full swing is more exciting at first. Being able to hit a golf ball farther than Barry Bonds could hit a home run is addictive.
- You start a hole with a tee shot, and although the stats show that there are more short-game shots than tee shots, the tee shot sets the tone for the hole. You are either in great position ready to attack the hole, or you in trouble looking to salvage the hole.
- Working on the short game can seem boring compared to a solid full shot.

So how can you change your thinking? How does the short game earn its rightful spot in your practice regimen?

It's time to set aside that adrenaline rush you get from jacking a thunderous drive and focus on a different kind of pleasure: The pleasure of saving strokes. Lower scores will be your best reward. It's time for you to take control of your game. And it starts in close. You want red numbers? Master the Red Zone.

By using Athlon's Red Zone Short Game Skills Test, you can accurately assess your Red Zone proficiency—your strengths, your weaknesses, where you need to get better. Our Red Zone scoring system allows you to evaluate your current skill level numerically, and it gives you a baseline by which you can measure your progress. Call this step the weigh-in before the diet begins. It can be painful, but it's necessary, and it's the first step in our 12-week road to improvement.

> **We want you to test and rate yourself in six categories:**
>
> **1. Wedges from 100 yards and in**
> **2. Bunker**
> **3. Pitching around the green**
> **4. Chipping**
> **5. Long putting**
> **6. Short putting**

1) Wedge Shots

For your wedge shots, place targets at distances of 20, 40, 60, 80 and 100 yards, then fire away. If you can't get your friends to serve as targets, use handy, visible objects like bag stands.

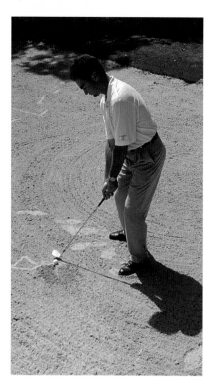

2) Bunker Shots

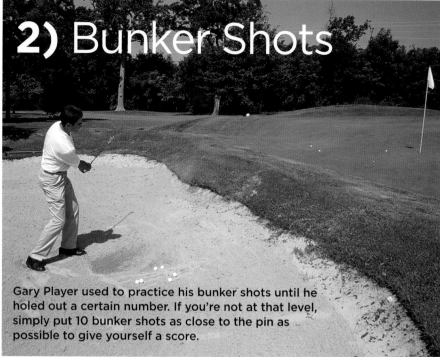

Gary Player used to practice his bunker shots until he holed out a certain number. If you're not at that level, simply put 10 bunker shots as close to the pin as possible to give yourself a score.

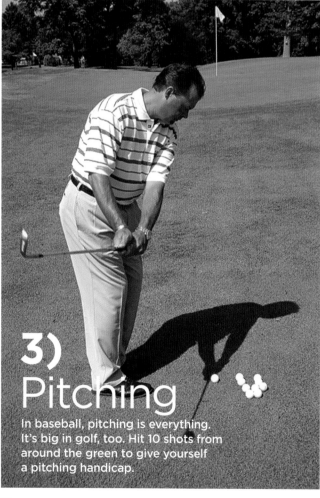

3) Pitching

In baseball, pitching is everything. It's big in golf, too. Hit 10 shots from around the green to give yourself a pitching handicap.

4) Chipping

Chipping can be your secret weapon. But first, figure out how much work you have to do. Hit 10 shots from the fringe and measure the results.

5) Long Putting

Unless you're a pro who's always firing at pins, lag putting from 20 feet and out is critically important. Hit two putts each from 20, 30, 40, 50 and 60 feet to give yourself a long putting score.

6) Short Putting

Holing those 12- to 15-footers can erase all kinds of mistakes. Grade your short putting by hitting two putts apiece from 3, 6, 9, 12 and 15 feet.

PURPOSE

To accurately evaluate your present skill level using a scoring system. This test allows you to have a measurable account of your progress.

DIRECTIONS

Using the test at the top of the following page, write in the score you have earned according to the scoring system for each Red Zone category. Then log your results on the accompanying chart to give yourself a handicap for each category. Using this systematic approach, you can create an efficient improvement plan and attack it aggressively. Then use the instruction from Rob and Charlie on the following pages to start chipping away (pun intended) at that handicap. Your scores will plummet while your confidence and efficiency from 100 yards and in will soar. Guaranteed.

The thing that really makes this test unique is that we give you a handicap in each individual category. As a golfer you understand what a 20 handicap is. With this test, you'll understand what a 20 putting handicap is, or a 30 bunker handicap. The ultimate goal? Lower your handicap, of course.

This may seem very simple, but quantifying your results is really a revolutionary concept in golf. Finding out just where you need the most improvement will result in less wasted time and more real progress.

Think about it. You may spend a lot of time on your game without seeing results on the course. You're probably beating balls on the practice tee when you should be honing your Red Zone skills. It's time you started working on the right stuff.

You might be surprised by what you discover. Many players might carry a 14 handicap, but they chip and putt more like a 30. The Athlon Red Zone skills test will reveal that and put you on the road to real improvement.

Using the following sheet, give yourself a score in each Red Zone area. Using this systematic approach and giving yourself a handicap in each area, you can create an efficient improvement plan and attack it aggressively.

SHORT GAME HANDICAPPING SYSTEM

PURPOSE: To accurately evaluate your present skill level using a scoring system. This test allows you to have a measurable account of your progress.

1) WEDGE SHOT – 10 SHOTS
(2 from: 20, 40, 60, 80, 100 yds)

where the ball lands, target can be a bag stand or range basket. You may need a partner or teacher to help you score where your ball lands.

SCORE		
*Hit target	3pts
0-10 feet	2pts
10-20 feet	1pt
20-30 feet	0pts
Over 30 feet	-1pt

2) BUNKER SHOT – 10 SHOTS
(From 7 to 15 yards; any lie - place the ball)

SCORE		
Holed	3pts
0-5 feet	2pts
5-10 feet	1pt
10-15 feet	0pts
Over 15 feet	-1pt

3) PITCH SHOT – 10 SHOTS
(15 yds. from edge of green, 10-15 yds. to cup, 25 to 30 yard shot total)

SCORE		
Holed	3pts
0-5 feet	2pts
5-10 feet	1pt
10-15 feet	0pts
Over 15 feet	-1pt

4) CHIP SHOT – 10 SHOTS
(From fringe - 5 from 45 ft. and 5 from 60 ft)

SCORE		
Holed	3pts
0-3 feet	2pts
3-6 feet	1pt
6-9 feet	0pts
Over 9 feet	-1pt

5) LONG PUTTING – 10 PUTTS
(To same hole; 2 from: 20, 30, 40, 50, 60 ft)

SCORE		
Holed	3pts
0-3 feet	2pts
3-6 feet	1pt
6-9 feet	0pts
Over 9 feet	-1pt

6) SHORT PUTTING – 20 PUTTS
(2 putts to same hole from 3, 6, 9, 12, 15 feet L-R)
(2 putts to same hole from 3, 6, 9, 12, 15 feet R-L)

SCORE	
Holed	2pts

TOTAL SCORE

Use the accompanying chart to log your scores and give yourself a Red Zone Handicap.

SHORT GAME HANDICAPPING SYSTEM

1. WEDGE	2. BUNKER	3. PITCHING	4. CHIPPING	5. LONG PUTTING	6. SHORT PUTTING	OVERALL HANDICAP
20=+5	20=+5	22=+5	22=+5	24=+5	26=+5	100-106=scratch
18=+3	18=+3	20=+3	20=+3	22=+3	24=+3	95-99= 2
16=scratch	16=scratch	18=scratch	18=scratch	20=scratch	20=scratch	90-94= 3
15= 1	15= 1	17= 1	17= 2	18= 2	18= 3	85-89= 4
14= 3	14= 2	16= 2	16= 4	17= 4	16= 6	80-84= 5
13= 4	13= 3	15= 4	15= 6	16= 6	14= 9	75-79= 7
12= 5	12= 4	14= 5	14= 8	15= 8	12=12	66-74= 9
11= 7	11= 5	13= 7	13=10	14=10	10=15	55-65=12
10= 9	10= 6	12= 8	12=12	13=12	8=18	44-54=15
9=10	9= 7	11=10	11=14	12=14	6=21	36-43=18
8=12	8= 8	10=11	10=16	11=16	4=24	29-35=21
7=14	7= 9	9=13	9=18	10=18	2=27	20-28=24
6=16	6=10	8=14	8=20	9=20	0=30	13-19=27
5=18	5=11	7=16	7=22	8=22		6-12=30
4=20	4=12	6=18	6=24	7=24		0-5=33
3=22	3=14	5=20	5=26	6=26		<0=36-39
2=24	2=16	4=22	4=28	5=28		
1=26	1=18	3=24	3=30	4=30		
0=28	0=20	2=26	2=32	3=32		
-1=30	-1=22	1=28	1=34	2=34		
-2=32	-2=24	0=30		1=36		
-3=34	-3=26	-1=32				
-4=36	-4=30	-2=34				
	-5=32	-3=36				
	-6=34					
	-7=36					

WRITE IN YOUR HANDICAPS BY CATEGORY

WEDGE	BUNKER	PITCHING	CHIPPING	LONG PUTTING	SHORT PUTTING	OVERALL HANDICAP

3

THE RED ZONE CHALLENGE

JACK NICKLAUS FACED

his 40th birthday in a surprising predicament: The game's greatest player, no longer able to hit it stiff at will, needed to find himself a short game. Even after two decades of dominance and 15 major championships, the Golden Bear realized

he couldn't do it alone. He needed a little help, so he summoned an old buddy from his past named Phil Rodgers, who taught the great Nicklaus a little pendulum chip. The result? Nicklaus won two majors in 1980, and in 1986 he gave golf fans their greatest thrill with his sixth Masters title.

Our point in all this: If a 40-year-old Jack Nicklaus needed direction to re-master his short game, do you think you can do it alone, through trial and error?

It's almost impossible to stumble upon a short game that you'll be happy with. Without directions, you're doomed to wander aimlessly until frustration drives you away from the course.

Well, we've got a destination in mind—and we've also got a set of directions on how to get you there.

We have created this system because golf lacks a clearly defined roadmap to success, and you deserve to have one. You need to know the things to do daily that will have the biggest effect on your game. As you will see, we are giving three different levels of time commitment depending on how busy your life is.

All we ask is that you stick with this for 12 weeks.

The 12-Week Challenge

So, before we get to the "How," let's quickly go over the "What." What do I need to commit to do to be a better Red Zone player?

In the chapters that follow, we'll be giving you all the information you need to improve your short game. In Chapter 12, titled 5 Minutes to Better Golf™, we give you simple daily exercises for putting what you learn into practice.

But what should you do with all this information? Here are three simple steps that answer that question.

Step 1

Decide on your level of time commitment. We recommend that you choose from one of three levels:

- **The Silver program** is a 1.5-hour commitment per week. That hour and a half includes daily drills (except for the seventh day) and one practice session per week at a short game area. This program is for the busy golfer who can squeeze one trip to the short game area per week and one and a half hours total per week into his or her schedule. The indoor 5 Minutes to Better Golf™ exercises are designed for everybody, but specifically for the golfer with limited time. If you consistently do your putting drills, posture and grip in the mirror, along with the impact exercises, you will see amazing improvement. Why? Because when you do anything consistently it becomes a habit.

- **The Gold program** is a 3-hour commitment per week. Your 5 Minutes to Better Golf™ exercises will be supplemented by two sessions at a short game area. The Gold program is for the golfer who can commit to three hours and two trips to the short game area per week. The Gold includes the same exercises as the Silver with more time and repetitions to make it second nature.

- **The Platinum program** is a 5-hour-plus commitment per week. This program is for the golfer who is looking for maximum results. If you want, you can build in fitness and strength training, tournament play and performance skills as well as your golf skills.

Step 2

Study the Essentials of the Short Game™ skills that we outline in Chapters 4 through 8. By focusing on what to do instead of what not to do, you will improve faster than if you used traditional methods.

Step 3

Go through the Commitment Process in Chapter 9 to make certain that you will follow through for the entire 12 weeks and beyond. When the "Why" is strong enough, we figure out how to do the rest. Then, follow our step-by-step instructions and have faith that this book includes the best short-game wisdom we have to offer, and that those who follow it will see measurable improvement.

Directions for the 12-Week Charts

Here, we outline the three commitment levels and the accompanying requirements. They're simple and easy to follow if you observe these recommendations:

1. The 5 Minutes to Better Golf™ in the chart refers to doing each of your most critical indoor drills six days a week.

2. When the chart refers to "Short Game area", that means that you are to pick a specific short game area and spend 30 minutes of practice time in that area.

3. For touch and feel, the more you can practice outside, the better.

4. Make an X on each day as you complete the task.

5. When you play, keep track of putts, up-and-downs from 40 yards and in, sand saves and up-and-downs from 100 yards and in.

" We have created this system because golf lacks a clearly defined roadmap to success, and you deserve to have one. "

The Athlon Red Zone Challenge
12 Week Training Schedule (Silver)

Week 1

M 5 minutes to better golf	T 5 minutes to better golf	W Short Game area, 5 minutes to better golf	T 5 minutes to better golf	F 5 minutes to better golf	S Play Golf, 5 minutes to better golf	S Off

Week 2

M 5 minutes to better golf	T 5 minutes to better golf	W Short Game area, 5 minutes to better golf	T 5 minutes to better golf	F 5 minutes to better golf	S Play Golf, 5 minutes to better golf	S Off

Week 3

M 5 minutes to better golf	T 5 minutes to better golf	W Short Game area, 5 minutes to better golf	T 5 minutes to better golf	F 5 minutes to better golf	S Play Golf, 5 minutes to better golf	S Off

Week 4

M 5 minutes to better golf	T 5 minutes to better golf	W Short Game area, 5 minutes to better golf	T 5 minutes to better golf	F 5 minutes to better golf	S Play Golf, 5 minutes to better golf	S Off

Week 5

M 5 minutes to better golf	T 5 minutes to better golf	W Short Game area, 5 minutes to better golf	T 5 minutes to better golf	F 5 minutes to better golf	S Play Golf, 5 minutes to better golf	S Off

Week 6

M 5 minutes to better golf	T 5 minutes to better golf	W Short Game area, 5 minutes to better golf	T 5 minutes to better golf	F 5 minutes to better golf	S Play Golf, 5 minutes to better golf	S Off

Week 7

M 5 minutes to better golf	T 5 minutes to better golf	W Short Game area, 5 minutes to better golf	T 5 minutes to better golf	F 5 minutes to better golf	S Play Golf, 5 minutes to better golf	S Off

Week 8

M 5 minutes to better golf	T 5 minutes to better golf	W Short Game area, 5 minutes to better golf	T 5 minutes to better golf	F 5 minutes to better golf	S Play Golf, 5 minutes to better golf	S Off

Week 9

M 5 minutes to better golf	T 5 minutes to better golf	W Short Game area, 5 minutes to better golf	T 5 minutes to better golf	F 5 minutes to better golf	S Play Golf, 5 minutes to better golf	S Off

Week 10

M 5 minutes to better golf	T 5 minutes to better golf	W Short Game area, 5 minutes to better golf	T 5 minutes to better golf	F 5 minutes to better golf	S Play Golf, 5 minutes to better golf	S Off

Week 11

M 5 minutes to better golf	T 5 minutes to better golf	W Short Game area, 5 minutes to better golf	T 5 minutes to better golf	F 5 minutes to better golf	S Play Golf, 5 minutes to better golf	S Off

Week 12

M 5 minutes to better golf	T 5 minutes to better golf	W Short Game area, 5 minutes to better golf	T 5 minutes to better golf	F 5 minutes to better golf	S Play Golf, 5 minutes to better golf	S Off

The Athlon Red Zone Challenge
12 Week Training Schedule (Gold)

Week 1

M 5 minutes to better golf	T 5 minutes to better golf	W Short Game area, 5 minutes to better golf	T 5 minutes to better golf	F Short Game area, 5 minutes to better golf	S Play Golf, 5 minutes to better golf	S Off

Week 2

M 5 minutes to better golf	T 5 minutes to better golf	W Short Game area, 5 minutes to better golf	T 5 minutes to better golf	F Short Game area, 5 minutes to better golf	S Play Golf, 5 minutes to better golf	S Off

Week 3

M 5 minutes to better golf	T 5 minutes to better golf	W Short Game area, 5 minutes to better golf	T 5 minutes to better golf	F Short Game area, 5 minutes to better golf	S Play Golf, 5 minutes to better golf	S Off

Week 4

M 5 minutes to better golf	T 5 minutes to better golf	W Short Game area, 5 minutes to better golf	T 5 minutes to better golf	F Short Game area, 5 minutes to better golf	S Play Golf, 5 minutes to better golf	S Off

Week 5

M 5 minutes to better golf	T 5 minutes to better golf	W Short Game area, 5 minutes to better golf	T 5 minutes to better golf	F Short Game area, 5 minutes to better golf	S Play Golf, 5 minutes to better golf	S Off

Week 6

M 5 minutes to better golf	T 5 minutes to better golf	W Short Game area, 5 minutes to better golf	T 5 minutes to better golf	F Short Game area, 5 minutes to better golf	S Play Golf, 5 minutes to better golf	S Off

Week 7

M 5 minutes to better golf	T 5 minutes to better golf	W Short Game area, 5 minutes to better golf	T 5 minutes to better golf	F Short Game area, 5 minutes to better golf	S Play Golf, 5 minutes to better golf	S Off

Week 8

M 5 minutes to better golf	T 5 minutes to better golf	W Short Game area, 5 minutes to better golf	T 5 minutes to better golf	F Short Game area, 5 minutes to better golf	S Play Golf, 5 minutes to better golf	S Off

Week 9

M 5 minutes to better golf	T 5 minutes to better golf	W Short Game area, 5 minutes to better golf	T 5 minutes to better golf	F Short Game area, 5 minutes to better golf	S Play Golf, 5 minutes to better golf	S Off

Week 10

M 5 minutes to better golf	T 5 minutes to better golf	W Short Game area, 5 minutes to better golf	T 5 minutes to better golf	F Short Game area, 5 minutes to better golf	S Play Golf, 5 minutes to better golf	S Off

Week 11

M 5 minutes to better golf	T 5 minutes to better golf	W Short Game area, 5 minutes to better golf	T 5 minutes to better golf	F Short Game area, 5 minutes to better golf	S Play Golf, 5 minutes to better golf	S Off

Week 12

M 5 minutes to better golf	T 5 minutes to better golf	W Short Game area, 5 minutes to better golf	T 5 minutes to better golf	F Short Game area, 5 minutes to better golf	S Play Golf, 5 minutes to better golf	S Off

The Athlon Red Zone Challenge
12 Week Training Schedule (Platinum)

Week 1

M	Short Game area, 5 minutes to better golf	T	5 minutes to better golf	W	Short Game area, 5 minutes to better golf	T	5 minutes to better golf	F	Short Game area, 5 minutes to better golf	S	Play Golf, 5 minutes to better golf	S	Off

Week 2

M	Short Game area, 5 minutes to better golf	T	5 minutes to better golf	W	Short Game area, 5 minutes to better golf	T	5 minutes to better golf	F	Short Game area, 5 minutes to better golf	S	Play Golf, 5 minutes to better golf	S	Off

Week 3

M	Short Game area, 5 minutes to better golf	T	5 minutes to better golf	W	Short Game area, 5 minutes to better golf	T	5 minutes to better golf	F	Short Game area, 5 minutes to better golf	S	Play Golf, 5 minutes to better golf	S	Off

Week 4

M	Short Game area, 5 minutes to better golf	T	5 minutes to better golf	W	Short Game area, 5 minutes to better golf	T	5 minutes to better golf	F	Short Game area, 5 minutes to better golf	S	Play Golf, 5 minutes to better golf	S	Off

Week 5

M	Short Game area, 5 minutes to better golf	T	5 minutes to better golf	W	Short Game area, 5 minutes to better golf	T	5 minutes to better golf	F	Short Game area, 5 minutes to better golf	S	Play Golf, 5 minutes to better golf	S	Off

Week 6

M	Short Game area, 5 minutes to better golf	T	5 minutes to better golf	W	Short Game area, 5 minutes to better golf	T	5 minutes to better golf	F	Short Game area, 5 minutes to better golf	S	Play Golf, 5 minutes to better golf	S	Off

Week 7

M	Short Game area, 5 minutes to better golf	T	5 minutes to better golf	W	Short Game area, 5 minutes to better golf	T	5 minutes to better golf	F	Short Game area, 5 minutes to better golf	S	Play Golf, 5 minutes to better golf	S	Off

Week 8

M	Short Game area, 5 minutes to better golf	T	5 minutes to better golf	W	Short Game area, 5 minutes to better golf	T	5 minutes to better golf	F	Short Game area, 5 minutes to better golf	S	Play Golf, 5 minutes to better golf	S	Off

Week 9

M	Short Game area, 5 minutes to better golf	T	5 minutes to better golf	W	Short Game area, 5 minutes to better golf	T	5 minutes to better golf	F	Short Game area, 5 minutes to better golf	S	Play Golf, 5 minutes to better golf	S	Off

Week 10

M	Short Game area, 5 minutes to better golf	T	5 minutes to better golf	W	Short Game area, 5 minutes to better golf	T	5 minutes to better golf	F	Short Game area, 5 minutes to better golf	S	Play Golf, 5 minutes to better golf	S	Off

Week 11

M	Short Game area, 5 minutes to better golf	T	5 minutes to better golf	W	Short Game area, 5 minutes to better golf	T	5 minutes to better golf	F	Short Game area, 5 minutes to better golf	S	Play Golf, 5 minutes to better golf	S	Off

Week 12

M	Short Game area, 5 minutes to better golf	T	5 minutes to better golf	W	Short Game area, 5 minutes to better golf	T	5 minutes to better golf	F	Short Game area, 5 minutes to better golf	S	Play Golf, 5 minutes to better golf	S	Off

The Athlon Red Zone Challenge
Customized Player Form

Fill out the following to create a customized daily plan and then follow your 12-week calendar.
Pick 2 or 3 drills for each short game category (read chapters 4-8 or refer to the 5 Minutes to Better Golf Drills in Chapter 12):

1) Short Putting
a. _____
b. _____
c. _____

2) Long Putting
a. _____
b. _____
c. _____

3) Chipping
a. _____
b. _____
c. _____

4) Pitching
a. _____
b. _____
c. _____

5) Distance Wedges
a. _____
b. _____
c. _____

6) Bunker Play
a. _____
b. _____
c. _____

The 5 Minutes to Better Golf™ Exercises you pick and record in the form above should be practiced 6 days a week during your 12-week Challenge. By practicing these things consistently for short periods of time you will see improvement and have a plan that you can stick with.

We recommend you get a 9-foot putting mat for the 5 Minutes to Better Golf™ putting drills you can do at home. You need to find a mirror or reflective surface so you can master the impact position and swing plane as well as some of the specific body movements in the pitch shot and bunker shot. We will have a list of recommended training aids in the appendix.

A 12 Week Example
Seven easy steps to better golf

1. Read this book through once to get the big picture.
2. Take the Red Zone test and convert it to a Red Zone handicap. You can do this yourself or with the help of a PGA Professional.
3. Read chapters 4-8 again and look at the concepts for each part. Then look at the drills that transform these areas into strengths instead of weaknesses. Set some handicap goals for each category.
4. Fill in the two or three blanks under each category on the customized player form with the drills you picked out from the chapters and from the chapter on 5 Minutes to Better Golf™.
5. Pick a time commitment—Silver, Gold or Platinum—and stick with that training schedule for the next 12 weeks.
6. Test yourself in individual categories randomly to see how you are progressing before you take the test again at the end of the 12 weeks.
7. Take the test again at the end of the 12 weeks, see how close you came to the goals you set at the beginning and celebrate.

THE ESSENTIALS OF A GREAT SHORT GAME™

NOW IT IS TIME FOR THE

details. In the next several chapters we will lay out the fundamentals of each short game shot and the drills that give you the feel of how to do each one. Our goal in this is not to be more clever than the other short game books in the past. Our goal is to create for you an overall understanding and plan that will lead to your improvement.

You don't just need the fundamentals. And a plan of daily exercises won't do much good without the essential principles. We want to give you the ESSENTIALS of the Short Game.

As we said earlier, we've heard students say, "I don't care about my short game until I can get on or near the green. I want you to help me hit it better." We understand that way of thinking.

But we are going to help your whole game. Starting with the putter and working our way out, we'll be giving you Essentials that will create improvement all the way up to your driver. The Essentials of putting transfer to better chipping, which transfers to better pitching and so on. Small swings and slower swings provide the best way to learn. That's why working on your short game has such a great overall effect.

At some point you will reach that level where you realize it is your short game holding your game back, and when you do, these are the Essentials that will help your game.

The first step in the learning process is eliminating the misconceptions that are hurting your game. To prepare you for our program of improvement, we want to get these out on the table and then eliminate them.

Then, when you get to Chapter 4 and start getting the right ideas for Red Zone improvement, you'll see that we've cut out the fluff and filler to give you Golf's Greatest Hits.

Updating Your Software
Golf's Fallacies, Misconceptions and Deadly Instincts

Just like having outdated software or a virus in your computer, misconceptions create problems with your brain's circuitry. We need to get rid of them. Not all of these are Red Zone-specific, but they need to be dealt with before serious improvement can become a reality.

Golf's Major Misconceptions
"You're lifting your head" or "You looked up"

This is the faulty belief that hitting a golf shot is simply hand-eye coordination. It is believed that if you don't make good contact, it is because you took your eye off the ball. Our comeback to this faulty idea is that staring at piano keys is not going to make you a good piano player. There are a lot of other elements that go into playing a piano other than watching the keys. This concept can also be applied to golf. "Seeing" the golf ball is only a small part of the entire swing. The hands, arms, wrists, and shoulders all must be trained to bottom out the club in the right place to produce solid contact.

Taking the club "straight back and straight through" will create straight shots

On the surface, this seems logical, but because we stand to the side, and the club is shaped the way it is, the shape of the swing is not straight back and straight through, but a circle tilted over, an arc. This concept relates to the master task of path/face combination, which you will read about in a following section.

"Keep the left arm straight"

There is a glimmer of truth in this because we are trying to maintain width in our golf swing; unfortunately, the concept has led to tension-filled golf swings.

"Keep the head still"

This directive in conjunction with "Keep the left arm straight" leads to a reverse pivot—a player's weight is on the front foot during the backswing and transferred to the back foot on the forwardswing.

"Effort/Muscle/Strength = Power"

You want effortless clubhead speed. Swinging harder and being stronger will not necessarily create greater distance in your golf swing. The correct formula is clubhead speed + solid contact = distance.

"Don't leave this one short" or "Make sure you don't kill it"

Misconceptions in putting are fewer and have more to do with our fears. Putting is the simplest act in golf, but not the simplest to master. Just look at the effect putting poorly has on tour players long-term. Losing touch on the greens has driven many great players to unique grips and long putters. Chapter 4 will give you a game plan to make this a strong part of your game.

Golf's 3 Deadly Instincts ...

So much of golf is contrary to what our instincts tell us. So, to get us started, let's look at what golfers instinctively want to do—but shouldn't do—when we swing a golf club. I know the word "deadly" sounds a little harsh, but so are chunking a ball into the water and skulling it across the green.

If a person walks onto a tee to hit a golf ball without any previous instruction, there are three deadly instincts that invariably take over. Left uncorrected, they create some bad habits. But once you identify and counteract these instincts, you will see vast improvement.

The deadly instincts: Scoop It, Steer It, Kill It

Here they are in order of "deadliness":

1) Golfers try to "lift" the ball into the air

Rather than "striking" the ball, golfers will try to "scoop" the ball into the air. With a scooping motion, the weight stays back, and the player hits on top of the ball or too far behind the ball. To make matters worse, the golfer is then told—incorrectly—that he lifted his head. With a bad diagnosis, you can't get better.

2) Golfers try to steer or guide the ball towards the target

Taking the club straight through to the target seems logical, but because we stand to the side, and the club is shaped the way it is, the shape of the swing is not straight back and straight through, but a tilted circle. The more you steer to hit it straight, the more crooked the ball goes.

3) Golfers try to kill the ball

When the instinct to "kill" takes over, bad things happen. Swinging with rhythm and creating effortless clubhead speed is the better way to achieve distance than exerting a lot of energy, but it certainly doesn't seem correct.

Now, let's replace these misconceptions and deadly instincts with the correct concepts, and get started on lowering your score.

4

PUTTING

> " There is no similarity between golf and putting; they are two different games—one played in the air, the other on the ground.
>
> Ben Hogan "

HOW IMPORTANT IS PUTTING?

Dumb question, right? Putting is so important that it has been described as a "game within the game." Another way to put it: The object of the game is to put the ball in the hole in the least number of strokes. Finding the hole is accomplished over 96% of the time with the putter. In other words—you complete your ultimate objective with the putter in your hands. It doesn't get much more important than that.

To putt well, you must accomplish two simple tasks. First of all, **roll the ball well**. Secondly, **roll it on line**. This seems obvious, but there are some psychological and visual barriers to doing these two things.

Barriers to Good Putting

1) The size of the hole
-The small diameter of the hole (4.25 inches) gives the golfer the feeling of having to be perfect.

2) Standing sideways causes a visual distortion
-When reading the putt from directly behind the hole you can see the line as it is. When you stand sideways as you address the ball, you are seeing a distorted image that may be fooling you.

3) Poor practice habits
- Haphazard practice leads to less than stellar results. By practicing in a way that insures success, you develop good habits and your confidence grows.

4) Fear
-Fear, anxiety and nerves—a time-tested recipe for poor performances on the greens.

Following our plan over a 12-week period is going to eliminate these barriers and let you focus on the Essentials of Putting™ outlined here.

Roll the Ball Well

Let's define this term a little more clearly: Rolling the ball well happens when the putter is swung smoothly, the ball is hit solidly and the speed takes the ball into or near the hole. Most of us have learned to putt with our only guide being the motivation and pressure of trying to make it. We need to shift the focus to a good stroke with good speed control.

Putting is perhaps more feel-oriented than anything else in golf, but there are some real-world techniques that you can use to take putting out of the realm of pure guesswork. Repeat these drills, and long putting will become almost as natural as walking.

Drills

1) Pendulum Drill — Swing the putter back and forth with a 'tick, tock' beat. Find a 20- or 30-foot putt and count an even 'tick, tock' to yourself as you putt the ball. Watch the ball roll all the way and notice if you hit it too hard, too easy or just right. Do this for at least five minutes to keep your focus on the pendulum feel. Over a period of 12 weeks this will become second nature.

Golfers have an innate sense of touch; they simply need something to draw it out of them. The "Look at the Hole" drill does it.

3) Right Hand Only Drill — When putting with one hand, golfers naturally swing the putter and don't guide the ball. This leads to a sense of truly rolling the ball and not over-controlling and guiding it.

Let the putter swing freely between your thumb and forefinger to get a feel for the natural tick, tock rhythm.

2) Look at the Hole Drill — One of our favorites. This drill is simple. Instead of looking at the ball as you putt, look at the hole. Free-throw shooters don't focus on the ball; they look at the hoop. Like basketball and other sports where you get a good sense of the target by looking at it, the same thing happens in your putting. After the first few awkward putts, most golfers notice they develop an uncanny sense of speed and direction. Golfers have an innate sense of touch; they simply need something to draw it out of them. This drill does it.

When you putt with your right hand only, it really forces you to swing the putter.

4) The "Don't Look" Drill — This drill forces you to take the feel of the other drills and put it to the test. Find a spot 30 to 40 feet from the cup and putt the ball toward the hole. Before you look up, you must guess how far the ball is from the hole in terms of distance and direction. If you are correct or close, you have drawn out your feel of how far to hit the ball. This is sometimes referred to as the 'mind's eye.' You will find that this drill will help you get better and better at feeling how far to hit the ball.

5) The Shadow Knows — Moving your head while putting can lead to a variety of problems, but there's a simple way to train yourself to keep your head still. Position yourself so that the shadow of your head falls over some point of reference, like the hole. Then watch your shadow while you make some practice strokes. If your head moves during your stroke, it will be obvious to you (photos C and D). Practice your putting stroke while keeping your head's shadow positioned over the reference point, and you'll learn to putt with your head still (photos A and B). Simple but effective.

Do these drills as we prescribe in the Challenge and you will watch your ability to roll the ball get noticeably better by test time and, most importantly, on the golf course.

Before you look up, try to picture how close to the hole the ball is. This will help your feel immeasurably.

Yes: Your head's shadow stays over the hole

No: If your head doesn't remain still, your shadow will let you know

Roll the Ball On-Line

This is the more detailed part of putting, and it's received most of the ink—how to grip, stand, line up, etc. These things are also essential, but having a fundamentally sound stroke and not knowing how to 'roll' the ball is a big mistake. The following Essentials will help us in our quest to start more putts on line. Match these essentials with the 'feel' you learned in the previous section, and you'll be draining 20-footers.

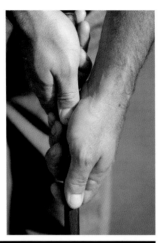

Left: Reverse Overlap Grip. Right: Left Hand Low Grip

Putting Essentials™

1) Grip and Setup — The Essential in gripping the putter is to create a proactive relationship between your hands and the putter face. Many different grips have worked over the years, but there is one Essential that these successful grips have all had in common: They all square the clubface at contact. Here, we show you the reverse overlap grip, which is the most common, as well as the left-hand low grip.

Our Setup Essential is designed to create a consistent arc and path for the putter.

1) Bend over from the hips
2) Eyes slightly inside the target line and behind the ball
3) Hands and arms hang right below the shoulders
4) Shoulders and forearms are parallel to the target
5) Forearms are in line with the shaft
6) Ball position in front of your dominant eye
7) Maintain grip pressure

2) Face Control — The face must be pointed at the intended target to get the ball to go there. We know that statement seems obvious, but it is surprising how many people don't play or practice as if the face angle is the most important factor. In our drills section you'll find the best and most effective drills for making this into a strength.

3) Speed Control — This is what we talked about earlier. Assuming reasonable path, face and centered hits, you need to hit a putt and then adjust by feel. Our goal is to "unlock" your feel with a series of drills. Don't change mechanics or agonize over it. Trying to be perfect on every putt leads to tightness and is a roadblock to your feel. Let the brain feel a long putt and a short putt, and it will calculate the middle between the two. It becomes more like tossing a ball.

4) Hitting the ball on a consistent spot on the clubface — It is important to hit the ball on the same spot on the putter every time so you know how the ball will react off the putter. Notice that we said the "same" spot, not necessarily the "sweet" spot. We recommend the sweet spot, but we also understand why Isao Aoki is a good putter. His ball reacts the same way each time even though he is hitting the ball with the heel of the putter.

5) Aim — Aligning in putting is inherently more difficult because we have to stand sideways. This creates a distorted image as we look at our target. To become proficient at lining up, we suggest you use training aids such as the chalk line, the stakes and string and the credit card drill.

6) Path — Your putter has at least a 10-degree angle by the rules of golf. This angle must be taken into account when swinging the putter most efficiently. On short putts, there may be an appearance of straight back and straight through. There is still an ever-so-tiny arc. Later in the chapter we list the best drills and training aids to perfect your path.

7) Swing the club — The to-and-fro motion that comprises a swing is necessary even in a small putting stroke. The rhythm and flow of a swing breeds consistency in your putting. The Pendulum Drill from earlier in the chapter is designed to help you develop this Essential.

As we turn to the drills, you'll notice that we've referenced the applicable putting essentials with each drill. Use these notations to maximize your practice time.

1) Putting String

(Essentials 2, 5, 6)

This is one of our favorites. You can work on improving straight putts and breaking putts. This aid helps your path, face control and a pattern of success for confidence. Affix a length of string to two pencils, then stick the pencils in the ground so that the string is taut. Place the ball underneath the string, then use the string as your guide.

2) Your Credit Card Can Make You Money

(Essentials 2, 5, 6)

A

A: Find yourself a straight-on 8-foot putt. Once you think you've lined up correctly, have your buddy replace the ball with a credit card. The card will tell you the exact direction your putter face is pointing. B/C: Place the ball on top of the card, and putt.

B

C

2) Your Credit Card Can Make You Money — Credit cards tend to get us in trouble financially, but we've found a way to get your credit card to make money for you.

The putter face must be pointed at the intended target to get the ball to go there, as obvious as that may seem. Lining up perfectly is difficult when you're standing sideways, as we do in putting, but there's a solution.

Find a straight putt from about 8 feet, and line up to the heart of the hole. When you think you are lined up correctly, move the ball away, pull out your credit card and align the edge of the putter with the edge of the card (It's better if you have a partner to line the card up for you).

Now, stand back and look at where the card is pointed. This will tell you if you're lined up correctly. If your alignment is good, keep doing what you are doing. If your alignment is poor, use the credit card as an alignment aid by lining it up to your intended target; then place a ball on the card and putt off the top of it.

When you look toward the hole, you will get progressively better by seeing what straight really looks like. Then when you take the card away you will be able to line the putter up to the hole and take it there when you putt.

This simple drill will allow you to consistently control your face angle when putting and make those money putts. Use that credit card correctly, and people will start owing you money.

3) The Putting Plane

The putter is a club that's angled at least 10 degrees, so you need to make sure you're swinging the putter the way it was designed to be swung.

First, get a feel for the angle of the club by holding the blade flat in the palm of your hand (see photo at right). Compare that with holding the shaft perpendicular to the ground (photo below right).

See the difference? The angle of the clubface in relation to the shaft makes it necessary for you to swing the putter with a slight arc.

Too many players take the club straight back and straight through, which is not the way the putter was designed to be swung.

Using a device called an arc board can help you get a feel for the proper putting motion. With that slightly angled piece of metal as your guide, the putter gently goes back up and in (right, top), and after impact, it gently goes back in again (right, bottom).

One danger of this exercise: Don't exaggerate the arc motion. Don't go from one extreme—straight back and straight through—to the other—an exaggerated arc.

The Putting Plane I'm using in these photos is available at eyelinegolf.com

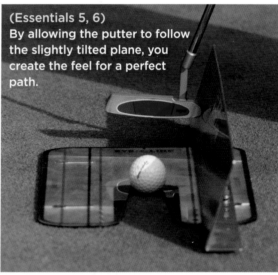

(Essentials 5, 6)
By allowing the putter to follow the slightly tilted plane, you create the feel for a perfect path.

4) Putting Mat

(All Essentials)
Watching the ball go in and creating a pattern of success is the key to the putting mat. Many of these drills in this section should be adapted to the mat.

5) Rubber Band Drill

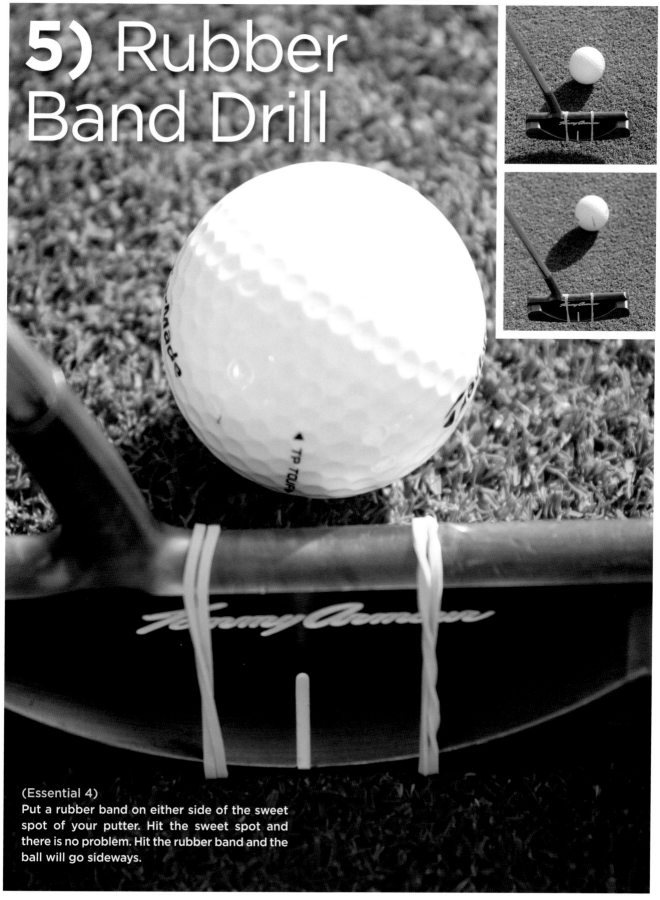

(Essential 4)
Put a rubber band on either side of the sweet spot of your putter. Hit the sweet spot and there is no problem. Hit the rubber band and the ball will go sideways.

6) Putting Laser

(Essentials 2, 6)

With this revolutionary aid, you can visually train yourself to correct your putting and shave strokes off your game. This putter allows you to feel for the first time what a correct, consistent putter alignment and stroke feels like.

By accurately positioning two laser beams—one allowing you to monitor the face alignment, and the other, the path of your stroke—you can see what perfect feels like.

My putter allows you to:
- Practice your putting with perfect alignment
- Monitor the path of your stroke backwards and forwards
- Monitor the putter face during the stroke
- Find out what a correct alignment and putter path and face feel like
- See any deviation or manipulation of the path and face throughout the stroke
- Repeat this process to exact terms
- Establish a muscle memory repeating stroke through daily practice

Available with green laser beams (my patented SOCRATES Putting Aide) or red laser beams (the PLATO Putting Aide—perfect for the Red Zone).

- Rob Akins

7) Metronome

(Essentials 3, 7)
Listening to and emulating the steady beat of a metronome will help you develop the tick-tock rhythm we talked about earlier.

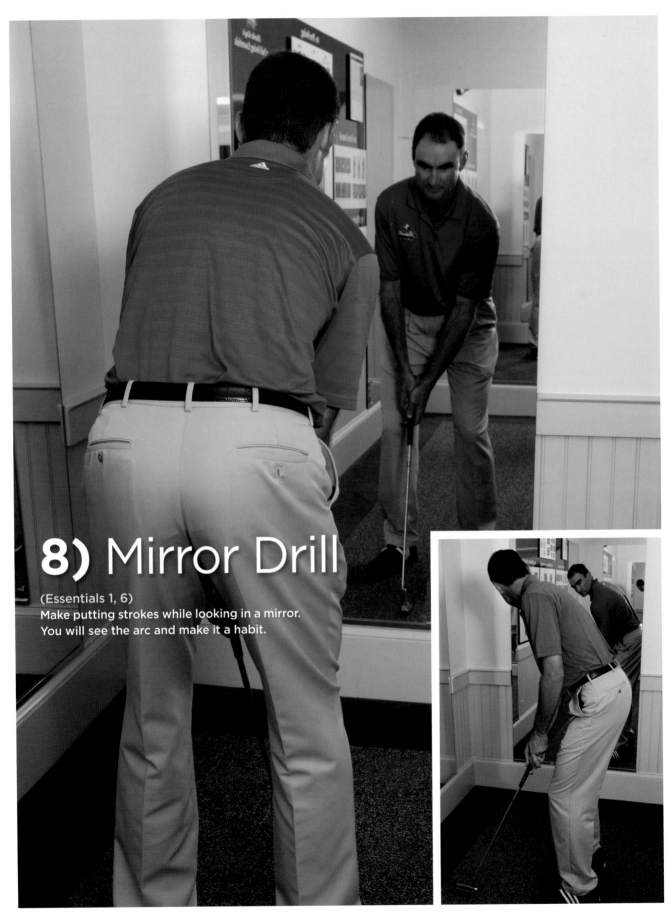

8) Mirror Drill

(Essentials 1, 6)
Make putting strokes while looking in a mirror.
You will see the arc and make it a habit.

9) Metal Ruler Drill

(Essentials 2, 5, 6)
This is a great alignment drill. Place a metal ruler on the ground pointing to the hole on what you think is the proper line. Then place the ball at the end of the ruler and putt. The results will reveal any alignment flaws.

Challenge Drills
Use these drills to hone your competitive skills:

2) Indifference Drill — Putt 5 balls into the hole from one foot, 4 from two feet, 3 from three feet, 2 from four feet and 1 from five feet. Then go in reverse, 1 from five, etc. If you can make it from start to finish without missing, you are done. Many golfers get ahead of themselves and miss a short one. It forces you to stay focused.

3) Around the Horn — This drill was designed by Dr. Rick Jensen. Find a hole that has enough break from the side angles that you have to play the ball outside the hole. Putt from three feet at four spots equidistant around the hole, then four feet at all four spots, then five feet at all four spots. Starting at three feet, make three putts in a row and then move to the next spot. As long as you don't miss, you keep moving to the next spot. If you miss, you must start the goal of making three in a row again. You keep track of your total number of misses. When you have finished from the last five-foot spot, you have your total number of misses. The Tour norm for the best putters is two or three total misses.

4) Red Zone Putting Tests — Periodically take this portion of the Red Zone skills test to see how you are progressing.

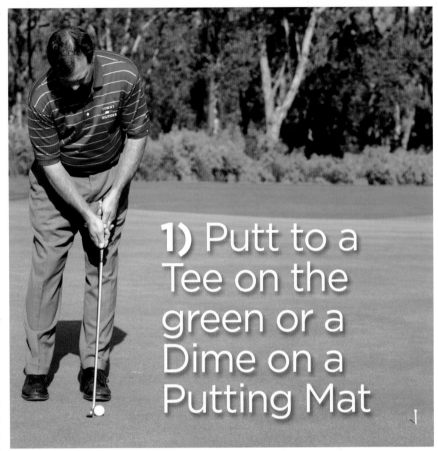

1) Putt to a Tee on the green or a Dime on a Putting Mat

By selecting a target that's even smaller than the hole, you learn superior focus and precision on the greens. This one is Rob Akins' personal favorite.

Speed vs. Line

They're the two most important elements of putting, but they often seem to conflict with one another as an amateur approaches his putt. On the longer putts, amateurs often worry too much about the line and totally misjudge the speed, leaving themselves with a tough second putt. Then, when they stand over that second putt, they often worry so much about the speed that they forget to judge the line properly. The result? Way too many three-putts. Sound familiar?

I want you to reverse your thinking as you stand over your putts. On the longer putts, especially those of 15 feet or more, the speed is much more important than the line. Instead of worrying so much about the line, I want you to envision a path to the hole that's 8-10 inches wide, and to play maximum break. The speed is the critical thing on those long lag putts. This approach will leave you with much more makeable second putts and curtail those dreaded three-putts.

When you get close, reverse that thinking. The shorter the putt, the less you focus on the speed. Here's where you get precise with the line. Pick a small speck where the ball will drop into the hole. You might even want to take some of the break out of the equation on the short putts.

Putting is a mental exercise. If you train your mind to approach it properly, you'll be amazed at the results.

Remember. . .

- On the long putts, envision a wider path to the hole, play maximum break and focus on the speed.
- On the short putts, concern yourself less with the speed and focus on the line, maybe even taking out some of the break.

Control the Speed, Control the Distance

A wise man once told me that the Golf Gods you always hear about go by the Eastern-sounding names of Tem-po and Ti-ming.

The tempo of your stroke is critically important on the putting green. If you can master it, you can control the speed and the distance of your putts.

Long Putts

On long putts, your goal is not necessarily to hole the putt (although that's always nice). Your goal is to putt the ball within tap-in range, and that means distance control. By grooving a smooth, consistent takeaway, you can develop a feel for how far back you need to take the putter. The length of your backswing determines the distance the ball will roll.

Shorter Putts

On shorter putts—putts that you fully intend to hole—the speed is the key, and the backswing again is the determining factor. Practice enough to know how long your backswing needs to be to hole those six-footers.

REMEMBER:
- The length of the back stroke determines the putter speed on the forward stroke, and thus the distance the ball will roll.
- The back stroke and through stroke should be equal in length. This is where the putting stroke does resemble a pendulum.

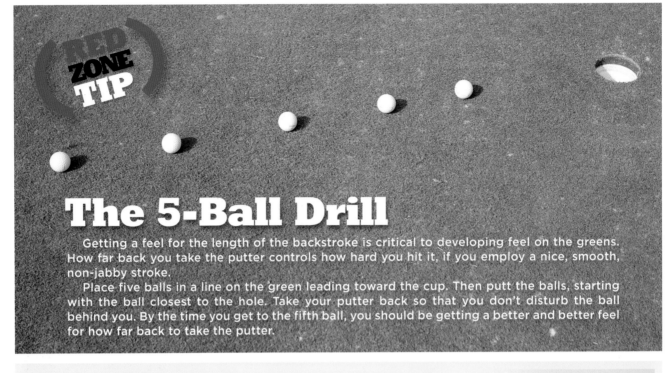

The 5-Ball Drill

Getting a feel for the length of the backstroke is critical to developing feel on the greens. How far back you take the putter controls how hard you hit it, if you employ a nice, smooth, non-jabby stroke.

Place five balls in a line on the green leading toward the cup. Then putt the balls, starting with the ball closest to the hole. Take your putter back so that you don't disturb the ball behind you. By the time you get to the fifth ball, you should be getting a better and better feel for how far back to take the putter.

(RED ZONE TIP) On Track

Do you find yourself nervous on the short putts? When we get nervous, it creates a tentative, shaky stroke. Here's a drill that can help. And it proves that you don't have to be perfect, which is good news for all of us.

Take two clubs and create a track between your ball and the hole. To hole these short putts, just try to keep the ball between the tracks, because this is a much easier task than trying to putt to a precise spot. If the speed is right, then the size of the hole increases.

Trying to be too precise or perfect leads to tentative strokes. This drill can be invaluable. Once you realize you have more room for error, you can putt freely.

(Left) This grouping of balls shows the five different tracks the ball can take to the bottom of the cup—provided the speed is right. You don't have to be perfect; just commit to one of these tracks, then execute a smooth, steady stroke.

How Shoulder Movement Affects Path

Many of you probably don't realize the big effect your shoulders have on your putting stroke. A big shoulder swing on your putting stroke makes the putter face go in and out, and you end up cutting across the ball, much like a slicer does off the tee. You can compensate by adjusting your line, but why not just do it right?

Here's how: Keep your head and your lower body still, and train your shoulders to support the slight arc along which the putter travels back and through the ball.

You'll notice in the first sequence that Mark's shoulders are moving left, his head is moving, and he cuts across the ball. We want the shoulders to support the slight arc path that the putter takes back and through the ball.

In Charge

Don't just leave the putter face down there to fend for itself. I want you to put your right hand in charge.

Picture your right hand as the equivalent of your putter face. Get used to the notion that, if your right hand is pointed toward your intended target, the ball will go in.

Another option: Left hand low. Some players prefer to make their left hand the lower hand on the putter, putting that hand in charge of the stroke.

Either way, your putting stroke will have more authority, and your putts will fall with greater frequency.

Put your lower hand in charge of your putting. For most players, that means the right hand (above, right). But the left hand-low grip (above, left) is a viable option, as long as you put that hand in charge of your putting stroke.

Practice may NOT make perfect

Does this sound like your putting routine? You address the ball, then take a few practice strokes. Then, when you actually hit the ball, you've lost the vision you had when you first surveyed the putt.

Here's my advice: Read the green, see the speed, then the line, get that picture in your mind, then walk up and hit the putt. If you want to take practice strokes, do it before you approach the ball and address it. Try putting without practice strokes and trust your initial vision of each putt. I bet you'll putt better.

1 Read the Green

2 See the Speed

3 See the Line

4 Make the Putt

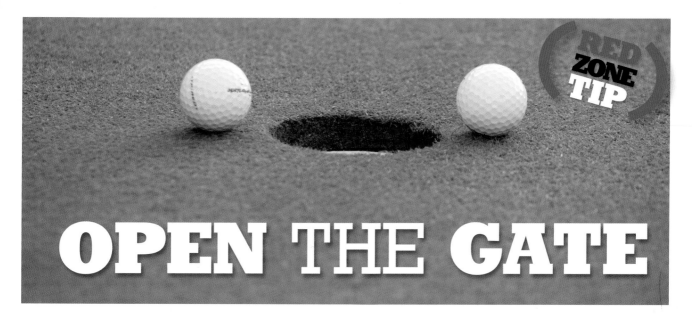

OPEN THE GATE

On the green, the hole can appear to be so small that players get very tight when it comes time to hit the putt, and they try to steer it. I recommend a very simple drill to overcome this tendency: Put a ball on each side of the hole, and think of that as the gate that you have to go through. This simple trick makes the opening look bigger, and it will help your confidence tremendously.

Instead of having to hit on that perfect straight line, which leads to stiffness and tension, this will allow you to relax and think, "I can get the ball into that opening. No problem." Try it and see if it doesn't improve your confidence and your putting stroke. In putting, as in life, the perfect is the enemy of the good. You don't have to be perfect on the green, just good enough.

REMEMBER — on a breaking putt, you'll need to shift the gate (above).

(RED ZONE TIP) Follow the Stripe

Vision is critical in putting. Your hands are going to tend to go where your eyes tell them to go. When you stand over a putt, your eyes are telling you a direction to hit the ball, but often your eyes are fooling you, because they're giving you a distorted image.

You've probably seen your favorite Tour players line up putts with the stripe on the ball pointed in the direction they want to hit the putt. You can follow their example.

Be aware of this, though: Once you've lined up the stripe on the proper line, it may not look like it's lined up properly once you stand over the ball. You can fix this problem, too.

Take your head and tilt it to the left; the stripe will look like it's pointed to the left. Tilt your head to the right, and the stripe will look like it's pointed to the right. Put your head more behind the ball, and the perspective changes again. I want you to adjust your head until the stripe appears to be pointing on the proper line. That's your new head and eye position for putting, because it gives you the true visual image you need as you strike the putt.

Once you've lined up the putt with the stripe pointed in the proper direction (opposite page), and you've addressed the ball, I want you to adjust your head, as I'm doing in these photos, until the stripe appears to be pointing on the proper line. That's your new head and eye position for putting, because it gives you the true visual image you need as you strike the putt (below).

(RED ZONE TIP) Learn from Lefty:
Practice those short putts

Phil Mickelson's work with the flat stick deserves a lot of the credit for his major success. You can learn from Lefty's approach to putting.

So how did Phil Mickelson win three majors over a nine-major stretch after going for so long without winning one? What's the story behind the story?

One anecdote about Lefty that you might have heard, but that you need to hear again, concerns Phil's ability to hole short putts.

Mickelson had a putting green in his backyard growing up and was regarded throughout his junior and college career as a great putter and chipper and a player who possessed great imagination and great feel around the green. But he knew he could be better.

Some time ago he enlisted the help of a great putter and teacher named Jackie Burke at The Champions Club in Houston. When Phil asked Jackie for his input, Jackie told him that he didn't put in the time in practicing putting that he should to win majors, and that he missed too many short putts.

Phil was a little taken aback by this. He replied that he worked many hours on his short game. Jackie proceeded to tell him that a lot of those hours were wasted. Phil wasn't quantifying his practice, and so he couldn't tell if he was improving, and he didn't know what he needed to work on.

Jackie gave Phil a piece of advice: He told him to practice his short putts until he could hit 100 consecutive three-foot putts around the hole. He told Mickelson to place balls around the hole like the numbers on a clock, then to circle the cup, holing one three-footer after another.

Phil replied, "But Jackie, I can do that now." But Jackie told him, "I don't think you can. You don't win majors because you don't putt as well as you think you putt."

Mickelson took the challenge and marched out to the putting green. He missed putt No. 20, and Jackie's point was made.

Mickelson left to go home and practice. A month later he called Jackie excitedly and said, "I did it! The last two days I've made 100 in a row."

When Mickelson embarked on this practice regimen, it would take him hours to hit 100 three-footers in a row. Now he does it every morning before he plays.

When I walk out on the practice green at a tournament, I can see where someone has worn a path around a hole at a three-foot radius, and I know Mickelson has been there.

In my mind, this has been one of the biggest development that has allowed him to win three majors. He's much better at holing short putts.

You can apply this approach to your own practice regimen. You might find that trying to hole 100 putts is way too frustrating. Try holing 20, then move to 30.

I was told that Tiger Woods is in the habit of making 100 six-footers in a row. Might be a clue as to why he's won so many majors.

– Rob Akins

"How" to Practice Putting

1. After reading the chapter, pick at least two drills to consistently do indoors and two or more to focus on outdoors.
2. The indoor drills are what we call 5 Minutes to Better Golf™ exercises. Spend 5 minutes or more doing these six days a week during your Challenge.
3. The outdoor drills will be practiced a little longer depending on which time commitment you choose.
4. Do the individual test from time to time to challenge yourself and check your progress.

Recommended Drills Prioritized for:

PROGRAM	ROLL THE BALL	TRAINING AIDS	GET THE BALL ON-LINE
Silver	1. Look at the Hole 2. Pendulum Drill	1. Putting Mat 2. Putting Laser 3. Putting Plane	1. Putting String 2. Credit Card Drill
Gold *All the above plus*	1. Right Hand Only	1. Metal Ruler 2. Metronome 3. Rubber Band Drill 4. Mirror Drill	
Platinum *All the above plus*	1. Don't Look Drill	1. All the Challenge Drills	

Reading the Greens

The main thing with reading the greens is experience. The more you putt and observe, the better you will become at reading greens.

1) **Always watch the ball roll until it stops.** Many amateur golfers make the mistake of not watching the ball all the way until it stops. The more information you brain has, the better it can calculate for the future.

2) **Look at the putt from below the hole to get a better read.** If all you do is look at the putt from behind the ball, you are missing some vital information. Looking from all around is typically unnecessary and hurts speed of play, but looking from below the hole is must.

3) **Visualize.** To be able to see the putt in your mind before you actually putt it is very important. Putt in the morning with dew on the greens so you can see the line the putt took. Putt while looking at the hole, as we advised earlier, to see the putt roll toward the hole and how it moves.

These are a few key ideas that help you read the greens. This will become a more important topic as your stroke develops.

The Three **Traits of a Good Putter**

1) You can see where the putter face is pointing.

2) You've got a great sense of touch and feel.

3) You've got proper shoulder movement.

RED ZONE SUCCESS STORIES

Michael Merrill

MICHAEL NEVER THOUGHT HE would become a Golf Professional nor did he really know the difference between a 3 iron or a 7 iron when he graduated from Gettysburg College and went to work in Boston for a career wearing a suit and tie. He was introduced to the game by playing occasionally with friends here and there and was quickly drawn to the challenge of shooting low scores and the effortless look of hitting a ball 300 yards. The other reason golf was a lure for him was the emotional letdown of not competing athletically anymore after growing up with thoughts of becoming a major leaguer and playing just about every other sport there is—except golf.

He decided to abandon whatever it was he thought he wanted to be, and through John Ronis, went to work at the Wayland Golf Shop in Newton, Mass., as a sales person. Initially the experience was similar to being dropped off in the middle of China, but he began to quickly catch on to the lingo and verbiage he needed to become a factor in the shop. He could not get enough golf, and he would play almost daily that initial summer. The Wayland golf course was a short drive away, and he would put the first ball in the air everyday and then get back to the golf shop by 9:00am. His average score was around 100 with an occasional high 90s round. At this stage he had had a couple of lessons from John, and his mind was made up that his future lay in the game of golf.

That fall he arrived in Casselberry, Fla., for his first semester at The Golf Academy of the South to begin a 16-month golf management program. "My friends and family thought I had gone off the deep end when informed of my plans, except for my mother—I could be a bank

followed led to his shooting a 75 only eight months later at a Monday Tournament. "I followed this plan closely and with a lot of dedication and energy. I have had my share of big numbers since then but I went on to become a PGA member and a Head Golf Professional.

"The message was clear and simple from Charlie that the golf swing is like any other motor skill—it is a process, not a secret. The short game was the focus of my efforts early on, and it was clearly stated by Charlie that the foundation must begin here in order for the development of my full swing to succeed properly. The plan also had to be measured and evaluated for it to be effective. Charlie's short game skills test was an essential part of my success, not only for the results but also for training to be able to execute under pressure. My overall score initially on the golf course did not come down rapidly, but I start-

His average score was around 100 with an occasional round in the high 90s. At this stage he had had a couple of lessons from John, and his mind was made up that his future lay in the game of golf.

robber and she would think I should go for it." On the first day he was informed he would play in his first tournament that Monday morning—9:00 shotgun start. "I had never competed in a shotgun tournament but had some experience with a shotgun hunting rabbits in Vermont," Michael laughed.

Monday arrived and he reported to he starting hole with the other 100 or so students who were at various levels in their training. "My turn arrived to hit the first tee shot and the feeling in my stomach was one I had never experienced before in sports. Little did I know that would be the first of 125 attempts I would make at the ball. I walked off the golf course that day feeling about as down and out as I ever been in my life. Looking back on it now the next thing that happened to me that was the greatest part of this story—I met Charlie King."

"Well, Michael, we have our work cut out for us, but it can be done," Charlie said as he mapped out the plan for Michael's improvement.

"Charlie was a teacher at The Golf Academy South and is to this day one of the best communicators I have met in my life," Michael said.

They structured the plan, and the map that Michael

ed to take solace in the fact that my testing numbers were improving. I give this test to my students at The Nantucket Golf School and it makes a substantial impact on each player to show the importance of the short game in the achieving the number one goal of all golfers-shoot lower scores. The relationship between the short game and the development of the full swing increases the value of this process of golf instruction. The 'two for one' benefit gained from a focused training program incorporating the short game leads to increased skill levels for all golfers—most important for new players the game."

Michael has been teaching golf now for almost ten years. "I base my success in golf instruction on this process that Charlie instilled in me early on. Looking back now I am one of the lucky people who take up the game of golf by starting with a teacher who is passionate and dedicated to reaching goals. I know the process Charlie and Rob have developed works based not only on my results but on the results of students. I continue to work on my golf game with Charlie and now have the opportunity to teach along with him for various programs. He is one of the few people I have met in this game who has one focus—getting people better at golf."

5 CHIPPING

WHEN I WAS IN MY TEENS

I had the opportunity to play and practice with Randy Simmons. You may not have heard of Randy, but he played at the University of Texas during the era of Tom Kite and Ben Crenshaw. Randy was a tremendous ball-striker who insisted that we hit a bag of 150 balls with each club in the bag—75 for him and 75 for me, with every single club. I made it pretty good through the short irons and mid-irons, but I was totally out of gas by the time we went through the long irons and the woods. I hadn't learned yet how to practice effortlessly—but that's a lesson for another time.

Then we would turn our attention to the short game and practice that just as hard. I'd say to Randy, "You hit the ball so well, why do you want to practice your chipping?" His reply: "Because I can be more aggressive when I know I can get up and down." We would start chipping, and many times Randy said to me, "When you're a good chipper, chipping gives you par for a partner." I've never heard it said better. If you can hit it near the green and are a good chipper, you can make a bunch of pars. In this chapter, Charlie and I want to give you par for a partner.

— Rob Akins

We've all admired great players like Raymond Floyd and Jose Maria Olazabal, who chip the ball so well they seem to chip in more often than they make a long putt. Emulating them is easier than you think. As with putting, once you have mastered the technique, it is the feel that will lead to great chipping. And the technique is relatively simple and straightforward, as Floyd and Olazabal will attest.

> **When you're a good chipper, chipping gives you par for a partner.**

Chipping Essentials™

The majority of golfers try to lift the ball into the air with a scooping motion. The result: The weight is on the back foot and the wrists are bending upward. We will show you how to bottom the club out and use a striking motion with an arc very similar to your putting stroke. We want you to hit the center of the loft of your club to get the ball into the air. We don't want you giving in to the scoop motion and trying to lift the ball into the air.

The great thing about chipping is this: Learning to hit a chip shot correctly leads to better ballstriking throughout the rest of your game. Many players will break their wrist at the last second, which will result in that scooping motion and inconsistency with their chip shots. Two antidotes to scooping: Keep your hands ahead of the ball; and slightly de-loft the club. This motion will actually make getting the ball up in the air easier. You will finally be using the loft of the club correctly.

We teach the basics when it comes to chipping. When we see chipping instruction that is gimmicky, that's a sign that the teacher is in effect throwing up his hands and saying, "You can't get any better doing it the right way."

Well, we have too much respect for you to give up on you. We're assuming in this chapter that you can get better, and that you can do it the right way.

With that in mind, the keys to effective chipping are:

1. Have 70% or 80% of your weight on the left side of your body at address and keep it there throughout the swing.
2. Have the ball positioned middle to slightly back in your stance.
3. Hands slightly forward. The angle you set at address needs to reappear at impact.
4. Make a small arc with the club back and through.
5. Maintain consistent grip pressure throughout the stroke.

Oftentimes players will concentrate so much on keeping their head down, they will end up doing so too long, which restricts their body movement and encourages a scooping motion. We want you to arc up after you hit the ball, not flip the wrists up. A perfect arc both back and through is one of the secrets to great chipping.

Distance Control

Distance control and touch start with solid contact. Once you can consistently make solid contact on your chips, then you can begin to make better shots.

We recommend that you become the master of two clubs for your distance control in chipping. Use the sand wedge or pitching wedge for the short and medium chips; the 7- or 8-iron for the medium or long running chips. It is important to notice how far these clubs carry in the air and how much roll they get.

Solid Contact

Forget the one-foot putt for a second as the simplest shot in golf. Discounting the putter, the green-side chip shot is the simplest motion in golf. It doesn't take a lot of moving parts, and the swing is short. Simplest doesn't mean it's the easiest. You may be having trouble with this shot, as a lot of golfers do. I'm going to make it simpler.

The chip is defined as a low, running shot where a pitch is defined by more air time. The chip is the introduction to hitting a lofted iron. The manufacturer gave you a club that gets the ball airborne by the way it is designed as long as you hit the ball solidly. So that becomes our first goal in chipping: Hit it solidly. With that in mind we are going to get the arc of our swing to hit on or past the spot where the ball sits.

All the essentials of chipping make sense if you keep hitting the ball solidly in mind. The weight should be leaning toward the left foot, the hands are slightly forward, and the ball is just back of the middle. These setup factors all encourage a solid shot. I keep mentioning solid because that is a must before you can have distance control.

In the swing, let the club make an arc going back. Don't keep the club too low or pick it up too sharply. On the forward swing, you want to avoid the most common fault in golf: the "scoop." Make sure to bump the ball with the hands leaning slightly forward.

Rob's Rules
for Consistent Chipping

1. Land it on the green.

2. Land it as close to you as possible

3. Land it on a flat spot.

Solid Contact:
Drills

1) Line Drill
Brush the Grass

Take the tip of the club head and draw a line in the grass, or use tees to show the line where the ball will be. If you prefer, you can paint a line on the ground..

Make small chipping swings and brush on or past the line. When you can accomplish this, you are on your way to solid chips. Remember the arc swing.

2) The Punisher Club

Take the club you are chipping with, then take another club out of your bag and turn it over and hold the two clubs so the upside down club sticks out beside your left hip. When you chip the ball the goal is for the upside down club not to hit you in the side. If you scoop and the club hits you, that is your "punishment."

3) 2X4 Drill

Set a board perpendicular to where you are trying to hit the ball. Then place the ball about 8 inches in front of the board. This forces you to have a correct arc, because if your swing is too shallow you hit the board. This drill creates a perfect arc.

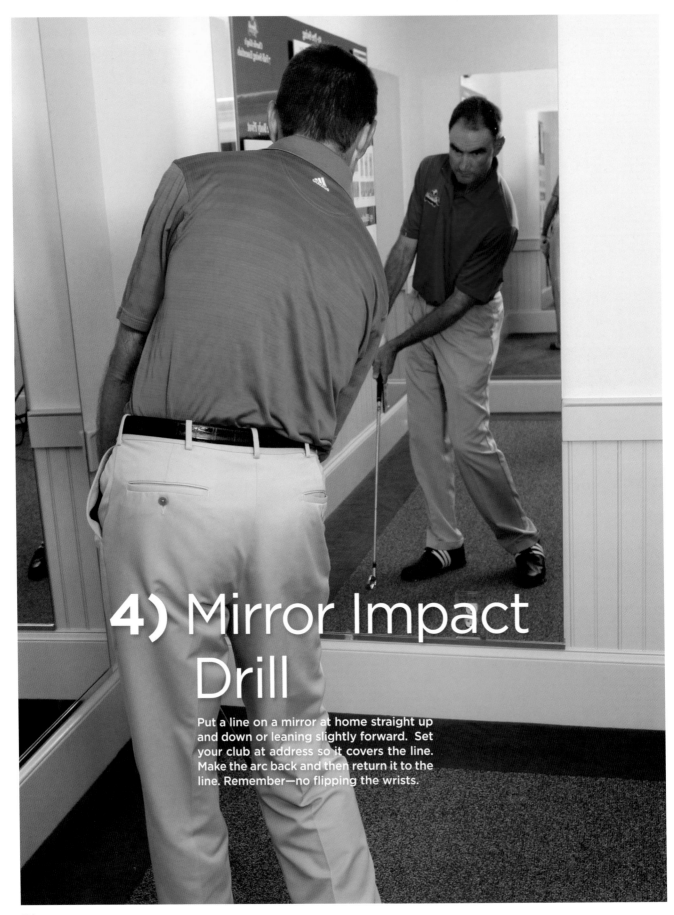

4) Mirror Impact Drill

Put a line on a mirror at home straight up and down or leaning slightly forward. Set your club at address so it covers the line. Make the arc back and then return it to the line. Remember—no flipping the wrists.

5) Look at Arms

Look at your arms and hands instead of the ball as you hit a few shots. This allows you to see if your wrist breaks down.

Touch and Feel:
Drills

1) Chip It In

Find a spot on the fringe 6-10 feet from the hole. Chip with the attitude that you are going to chip it in. Start to move farther away while maintaining the goal of holing it. This focus will increase your confidence and improve your results.

2) Ping Pong Ball

You can use this drill inside. Hit chip shots with a ping pong ball. Notice how hitting slightly down makes the ball go up and puts some spin on the ball. Be creative and take what you learn to the real ball. I have all my juniors and many of my adult players use this drill indoors. This drill teaches my players touch, the effects of spin and imagination. It also helps you develop your intuition when chipping—that's critically important. I used to chip ping pong balls onto my dining room table at home and try to get them to stay there. It's a fun, competitive little game to play with a partner, and one that really helps you learn to shape your shots. And while you've got the ping pong balls out, experiment with them. See what it takes to make them curve. Hit draws and fades. You can easily pick up little habits to take with you to the course.

— Rob Akins

3) Eleven Ball Drill

This drill was created by sports psychologist Dr. Rick Jensen. Chip 11 balls with the lie of the ball being wherever the ball drops. Chip to two or three different holes alternately until you have chipped all eleven balls. Take the five closest and the five farthest away which will leave you with the sixth ball, the median ball. Measure how far this ball is away from the hole and you now have your baseline. The Tour median is 1.5 feet. You work off of your personal best.

4) One Ball's Difference

Throw a sleeve of three balls onto the ground, and line them up facing the hole, one right next to the other. Line up as if the middle ball is normal ball position. Playing the ball that's farthest back will give you a lower shot with more run if you need it. Playing the forward ball will give you a slightly higher shot that will not run as much.

5) Take the Chipping Portion of the Red Zone Skills Test See page 14

> **Remember ...**
> 1. When the ball is coming off the face too "hot," check your ball position. You are normally playing the ball too far back in your stance.
> 2. When the ball is coming off the face too "soft," you are normally playing the ball too far forward.
> 3. Think of this shot as a bump and run. Hitting it solidly is the bump. You control the bump and then feel how the ball runs. With practice this can be one of your best shots.

THE ATHLON RED ZONE **69**

Two Clubs Are Better than One

MASTER TWO CLUBS
TO MASTER DISTANCE CONTROL

Distance Control

The chip is a low, running shot, while a pitch has more "hang time." Deliberately trying to lift the ball is your enemy if you use a club with loft. The manufacturer gave you a club that gets the ball airborne by the way it is designed—as long as you hit the ball solid. So that becomes our first goal in chipping: **Hit it solid.**

The next step is to have feel and control of your distance. There are two major theories on distance control in chipping. One says to become the master of one club, more than likely the sand wedge. The thinking goes that by using one club only, you will have better feel because you know the club so well.

The other theory is to have basically one swing and change clubs for different distances. As the shots get longer, you use a less lofted club like a 8-iron or 7-iron. The theory here is to create a formula for air time and run time using all your clubs, theoretically taking a lot of the guesswork out of distance control.

My suggestion? Blend these two theories. **Become the master of two clubs** and get the best of both worlds. Use your sand wedge or pitching wedge for the short chips, and your 7- or 8-iron for the intermediate and longer chips. This allows you to avoid the major drawbacks of the other two methods. The one-club method can be weak on the longer chips, and using too many clubs in your chipping can lead to inconsistency.

Think of this shot as a bump and run. Hitting it solid is the bump. You control the bump, and then feel how the ball runs. With only two clubs to master, you can become a great chipper.

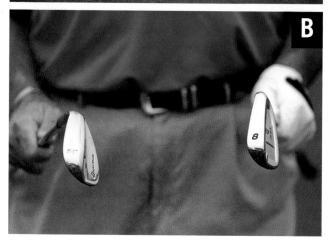

Use Your Head

Chipping is a critical part of the game. And there's more to it than simply how close you get the ball to the hole.

If you don't chip the ball in, you want to chip it to the right spot. Way too many amateurs approach their chip shots with some vague idea of getting the ball somewhere in the vicinity of the hole, with no thought for putting the ball in the right position. Then they're left with tricky downhill four-footers, and they end up three-putting—all because they didn't think when they stood over their chip shot.

When chipping the ball, ask yourself this question: If this ball doesn't go in the hole, where do I want it to end up?

Pros understand this. It's rare that they leave themselves with a downhill putt after a chip shot. They know that a downhill left-to-right five footer is a lot tougher than a 12-foot uphill putt. You're much more likely to three-putt from above the hole; from below the hole, you have a legitimate chance to one-putt, and the worst you're going to do is two-putt.

Simply by thinking your way around the greens, you can save yourself four or five shots per round.

CHIP & COUNT 123

Short chips and 4-foot putts tend to be difficult for golfers because of the perceived severity of the consequences of a miss. Golfers tell themselves, I shouldn't miss a 4-footer; I should get my chips and pitches really close. When that doesn't happen, they beat themselves up, adding to the struggles.

I want you to become a patient chipper. You can do this by chipping and counting.

Hit a chip shot, and as the ball travels toward its final destination, I want you to count how many seconds it takes the ball to come to rest. This will bring you to the realization that you can't get an immediate result.

When I see people chop and stab at their chip shots, they're trying for the immediate result—the ball close to the hole, right now.

Chip the best you can, then stand there patiently counting as the ball rolls, rolls, rolls and comes to a stop. Take that time as an opportunity to learn.

Watch the ball until it comes to rest. **Be patient.**

"

Watching the ball until it comes to rest is a great learning experience, but too few amateurs take the time to do it.

Charlie King

"

Lose the Loft Around the Green

Think back to the game's origins in Great Britain. Keeping the ball on the ground on a greenside shot has always been an option. Accomplishing that requires a less lofted club, be it a putter or a 3-wood.

Lately, the trend on these greenside shots has been to use everything from a 3-wood to a rescue club. Using this approach around the green allows you to employ a very wide-soled club, and that wide sole encourages the club to slide along the grass. And in turn, that wide sole discourages chili-dipping, where you stick the leading edge of the club into the ground.

Here's another bonus: The mass of that 3-wood or 5-wood requires less energy to get the ball from point A to point B than a putter. With a putter from off the green, players tend to leave the ball short. You're much more likely to get the ball near the hole with a 3-wood than with a putter, since it requires less effort and less energy.

To execute this shot, the shaft of the club should be vertical at address, like a putter, and you should hit the ball with the same motion as your putting stroke.

Rob Akins' Tour Talk

If you watch much golf this year, chances are good that some of the biggest shots in the biggest events will be executed near the green with a 3-wood or a rescue club. Some of these shots may even be career-defining shots.

Let me give you an example. My student and good friend David Toms has used the greenside 3-wood very effectively throughout his career, and one shot in particular was a career-changing moment.

It was at the 1999 International, and David, who had only one tournament win at the time, was clinging to a lead over David Duval, when he hit his second shot over the green on a par 5. He knew he needed birdie, but he had a bad lie and had to get the ball over a hump to get it to the hole.

So he grabbed his 3-wood and cozied the ball to two feet, allowing him to get that clinching birdie. It was a huge moment in his career and gave him the confidence to go out and win tournaments.

Sometimes, a lofted club by the green isn't the smart play. I want you to try a 3-wood when the situation calls for it.

Angle of Attack

Unless you hit every green in regulation, at some point you're going to find yourself faced with a downhill lie around the green. In such a situation, the first thing you need to do is to align your body with the slope. The angle of your shoulders is the key factor here.

If you don't adjust your body to the slope, you're prone to hit behind the ball or top it. Conversely, when you lean your body with the slope and get your shoulders fairly level with the slope (below), it allows you to hit the ball with a descending blow and catch it solidly. Because the ball tends to travel with a low trajectory, it's also a good idea to open the clubface a bit to give yourself more loft.

Here, I'm using my club to help me align my shoulders with the slope. By leaning along with the slope, I'll allow myself to catch the ball more solidly. Don't fight the slope.

Pick the Club You are Comfortable With

When you are on the golf course, especially in a pressure situation, pick the club and shot type that you are most comfortable with. Many golf pundits would chastise Phil Mickelson for using his L-wedge to hit a flop shot when the simple shot seemed to be a low running shot. It was the right choice for Phil because that was his favorite shot, and the shot he was most comfortable with. He had a better chance of pulling this shot off than any other.

Until you have had a chance to practice some of our techniques to the point they are second nature, use the shot you are most comfortable with. Little by little, put the new shots into your repertoire.

"How" to Practice Chipping

1. Use ping-pong balls or Almost Golf™ balls to practice indoors.
2. Pick your indoor drills and do them for short intervals for 6 days a week.
3. Do mirror work to make sure you have gotten rid of any "scooping" tendencies and have perfected an arc stroke.
4. Do your outdoor practice to targets and test yourself to monitor your progress. Use the chipping

Recommended Drills Prioritized for:

PROGRAM	SOLID CONTACT	TOUCH AND FEEL
Silver	1. Brush the Grass, Line 2. Look at Arms	1. Ping Pong Balls
Gold *All the above plus*	1. Punisher 2. 2x4 Drill	1. Take the Chip Test
Platinum *All the above plus*		1. Chip it In 2. Eleven Ball Drill

When Nancy entered the Golf Academy her handicap was around a 38, which tells you she was at best right around the national average for golfers.

NANCY HARVEY began her journey in golf playing recreationally with friends for a couple of years while she had a career in the business world. She didn't feel very fulfilled and decided in the fall of 1998 to enroll in the Golf Academy of the South (a two year occupational school for people seeking a career in golf). When she entered the Golf Academy her handicap was a around a 38, just above the national average for golfers in this country. Her first tournament she shot a 128.

At the Academy she met her first mentor and teacher Charlie King, as well as Brad Turner and staff. Her plan was to follow the management side of the profession. She didn't feel like she could ever be a good enough player to pass the player ability test to become a PGA Professional. During her 16 months at the academy the student-teacher relationship developed and grew. They worked on developing every aspect of her game, from long game, course management, and especially short game.

Nancy says, "One of the most dramatic experiences I went through was the short game skill testing. After the initial testing you can periodically test yourself to monitor your progress. It is a system that has measurable progress and improvement, it is not subjective, you either score better or you don't." She followed a program and had 100% improvement by the second testing.

This story almost didn't have a happy ending. In the fifth month she had a particularly bad tournament and was ready to quit. She saw Charlie for a scheduled practice. "I'm just never going to be good enough," Nancy said as she held back the tears. "Nancy, you are going have to trust me and have faith. I have taken so many people through this process, I'll tell you the only thing I've seen keep a person from getting it." "What's that?" Nancy questioned. "Giving up," Charlie shot back. "Have faith and trust me, you are going to get this."

The next several months saw steady improvement until Nancy had her crowning achievement. As she was a month or two away from graduating, she shot a 78 in a tournament. Fifty shots better than her initial tournament score.

Nancy now has a career in golf. Her handicap has gone from 38 to 6 and she is a member of the LPGA Club Professional & Teaching Division. "Charlie helped to develop my passion for the game and teaching others. He has developed and is constantly trying to improve on measurable ways of improving your golf game. The testing and measuring that Charlie taught me at the academy is the same things that I use today still. The short game improvements allowed me to score better on the golf course and bring my handicap down. I understand that's part of what he and Rob are using for the Red Zone Challenge. It's very exciting that they are bringing this secret to everybody."

6 PITCHING

ONE OF THE PEOPLE

who had a strong influence on my teaching was a golf professional named Harry Obitz. Harry was an innovator in the golf business. He was one of the first people to start a golf school in the late '60s— he called it Swing's the Thing Golf School. He had a golf show that toured the world, and he once even appeared on the Ed Sullivan Show.

Harry would come to Orange Lake C.C. in Florida for the month of January each year during his retirement, and I took that opportunity to pick his brain. There were many things he told me, but the one that stands out to me as influencing my teaching philosophy the most was when he explained to me about swing methods. He said, "Charlie, I don't ever want to hear that you became a method teacher. All swing methods are glorified pitch shots."

This was 1989, and there were three methods that had a lot of popularity. Harry took each one and did a pitch shot version of the method. When he had finished, he made his point: "Charlie, all a golf swing does is produce a ball flight. This is done because the skill and habits of the player, not because of a so-called scientifically better method. The problem with methods is that everyone regardless of their size has to fit into the same mold. But when you teach principles that build habits, a golfer's uniqueness can come out without sacrificing correct principles. So what I'm telling you is to teach principles, not methods." I heeded Harry's advice and what he called principles I term Essentials.

"All swing methods are glorified pitch shots."

The reason I feel this story is important to start this chapter is because if every method can be shown as a 'glorified pitch shot,' then learning to pitch the ball well not only helps your score but also gets you well on your way to a better full swing. It's our favorite two-for-one deal.
- Charlie King

Now let's map out the Pitching Essentials™ so you can improve on the golf course and lower your Red Zone handicap, while also improving your full swing in the process.

The Pitching Essentials™

1. The Pre-Swing
The pre-swing is made up of three key elements: GRIP, AIM, AND SET-UP (POSTURE AND STANCE).

Grip

First, to correctly hinge the club, you should take the grip-end of the club and hold it only with the heel pad (which is placed on top of the grip) and the forefinger. You should then move the club up and down to check if the club is hinging properly. When you wrap your remaining three fingers around the club, you should see two or three knuckles on the left hand. If you see four knuckles, the grip is too strong; if you see no knuckles or just one knuckle, then the grip is too weak.

Next, you should place your right hand on the side of the club. The way you put your hands on the club allows you to achieve the second function of the grip, which is to square the clubface.

Now, take the club to the top of your backswing. Your left thumb and the pad of your right forefinger should support the club. If you are doing this with your grip, you now have a correct, functional grip.

There is a misunderstanding about light grip pressure. We like to see that the pressure in the arms and wrists is light and the fingers are snug on the club. This gives us the best of both worlds: speed from light arm and wrist pressure and support of the club through snug fingers on the club.

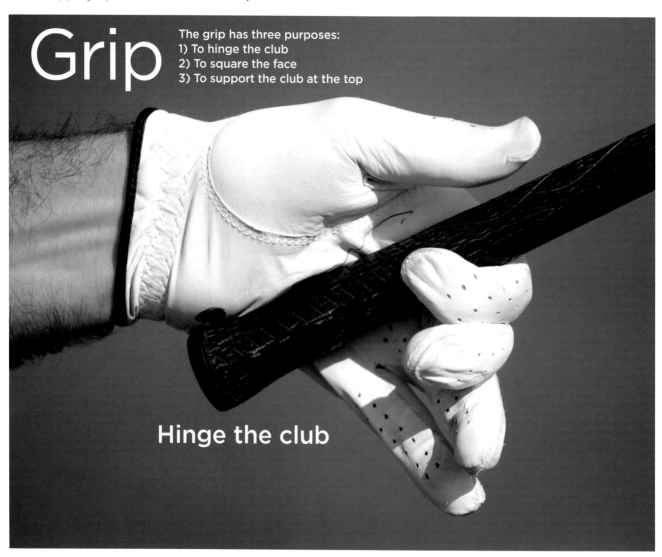

Grip
The grip has three purposes:
1) To hinge the club
2) To square the face
3) To support the club at the top

Hinge the club

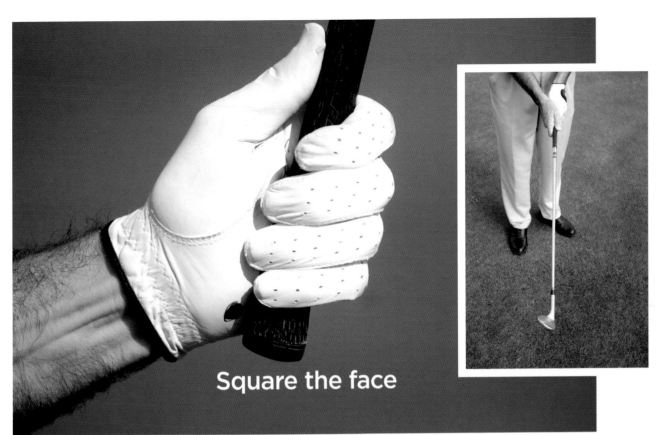

Square the face

Support the Club
at the Top

Aim

Many players set up with their shoulders lined up to the target. This is another one of golf's misconceptions because, in reality, the player is now lined up to the right of the target. Because the clubface hits the ball, it only makes sense that you should line up your clubface with the target. A key principle to remember when going through your pre-shot routine is "clubface first, body second." Another key concept to remember is the shoulders are lined up parallel to and left of the target. The lower body should be lined up slightly left to create resistance for the backswing. This resistance creates a stopping point. Because players are standing sideways and dealing with visual distortion, it takes practice and feedback to become good at alignment.

Set-up

RED ZONE TIP

The Anatomic Drill

Stand tall and let your arms hang to your side. I like to call this the anatomic state. This is how God designed you. Make a fist with your left hand and look down. You should see two or three knuckles. If your hand is on the club in that position, you have a better chance of squaring up the clubface more often.

— Rob Akins

Posture

Why is good posture important? Because bad posture has three devastating effects: It restricts your arm movement; it restricts your body turn; and it leads to injuries.

When you stand straight, the back has a very small "s-shaped" curve. When you have good posture, the spine is healthy, and there should be a small gap between the vertebrae. Between vertebrae there is tissue called a disc, which acts as a cushion. When your posture gets slouched forward, the vertebrae touch, and the discs get squeezed and pinched. When this happens and you take your backswing, the vertebrae are grinding on each other and pinching the discs. This happens shot after shot, for years. The discs get inflamed and the back pain kicks in. Eventually you are unable to play because the pain is so severe.

So how do we avoid this? Well, one of the main principles in the set-up is to bend from the hips, not the waist. If you bend from the waist, your spine will be in the unhealthy position we just described. You must also have a slight knee flex to keep your weight balanced. This will get you in an athletic, balanced position to start your swing. We check this by giving you the "push" test. Once you take your posture, we give you a light push forward and backward to see that you are centered and cannot be pushed over easily. This allows you to learn to "feel" correct posture and weight distribution.

When you grip the club, your right hand is slightly lower than your left hand; corresponding to this, your right shoulder should be lower than your left. This slight tilt of the upper body we call "secondary angle." This secondary angle should be maintained throughout the golf swing.

Stance

Your feet should be shoulder width apart for most shots. The rule of thumb here is that a stance that is too narrow will cause you to lose balance easily, and a stance that is too wide will restrict your turn.

Ball Position

The best place to start in describing correct ball position is with the bottom of the arc. Every time we swing, the circle of our swing will have a point where the club shaft is vertical. This is the bottom of the arc. For iron shots the clubs needs to be descending to hit the ball in the sweet spot and have the loft get the ball up. Therefore, the ball needs to be behind the lowest point for this descent. A driver, on the other hand, needs to be struck with the club traveling level to slightly up. This ball needs to be placed opposite this lowest point. The low point of a correct swing will occur under the left arm pit (because if the left wrist is correctly flat approaching impact, the shaft is vertical under the left shoulder). Our guidelines for pitching ball position are as follows:

1. Good Lie Pitch Shot – under the sternum.
2. Mediocre or Bad Lie – just back of middle

Use Ball Position to Control the Arc

In pitching, different distances call for different approaches. Depending on the amount of green you have to work with, your pitch shots may call for differing arc. Simply by using the ball position in your stance, you can control the arc and become a more accurate pitcher.

- When the ball is back in your stance, the arc is lower.
- When the ball is in the middle of your stance, the arc is a bit higher.
- When the ball is forward in your stance, the arc is highest.

Your position in relation to the ball also has an effect. The closer you stand to the ball, the lower the arc (below, left).

A: Note the three ball positions. The arc of the ball depends on where you are in relation to the ball.
B: The position of the ball in your stance affects the arc as well.

2. Clubface Control

This is the often-overlooked essential that significantly controls the direction of the golf ball. We know that where a ball ends up is predominantly controlled by the clubface angle at impact. We know statistically that most golfers slice and are under the misconception that it is because they didn't take the club down the target line. Most golfers have no awareness of where the clubface is during their swing, which contributes largely to miss-hits. Following are a few key checkpoints to determine if you have your clubface in the correct position throughout your swing:

No: Too Closed

No: Too Open

1) From the address position, take your club back to parallel to the ground with the toe of the club up (but angled slightly to the right).

Shut Clubface

2) Continuing the back-swing will allow the club to begin to hinge, and the leading edge of the club should be in line with your left forearm.

3) Now, when the club starts down, the leading edge will be in a neutral position.

4) Finally, the handle will be leading to hit the ball solidly and the face will be pointed toward the target. The ball jumps off the loft of the face toward the target as you follow through to the "toe-up" position.

Too many times players will make an exaggerated attempt to take the club straight through, leaving the face pointing to the right of the path, creating side spin that hits the ball to the right. With correct instruction on clubface control, slicing could be eliminated altogether.

Imagine the face of a tennis racket and how you direct the ball with the face pointed right, left and straight.

3. Striking vs. Scooping

Ball-striking is a term used to describe the quality of contact between the golf ball and the clubface at impact. To describe the difference between a "strike" and a "scoop," I like to demonstrate by having a student slap my hand with their right hand. Invariably the contact is solid and flush with my right hand.

With a scooping motion (above), the weight stays back and the player tops the ball or hits too far behind it. The proper motion is a strike (top), not a scoop. Note the position of the striker's hands just after impact.

Striking is the hands and handle leaning slightly forward at contact with the weight on the left side. The bottom of the arc will be at or past the ball for solid shots. In my opinion, this is the number one fault in golf and very few know it. When a golfer is overheard saying, "I lifted my head on that one" or being told, "Keep your head down," you know they are operating under this widespread faulty concept. What we call the Strike is the movement and position that is the key to solid golf shots.

— Charlie King

The problem is that players do not know how to correctly use a lofted club. Because of the scooping motion in an attempt to "lift" the ball that many players make at impact, the player will either hit on top of the ball or well behind it. A correct strike of the ball will result in consistent ball flight and greater distance.

4. Pivot and Secondary Angle

This is the slight tilt in the spine caused by the right hand being lower than the left on the golf club at address. This angle should be monitored and maintained for a correct pivot. The most common fault in a golfer's body motion is the reverse pivot. This has been caused over the years by golfers being told to, "Keep your head still" but not being told what to do with their body. We have found that keeping this slight tilt consistent throughout the swing simplifies the pivot and makes it efficient.

The pivot is the way your body moves in the swing. It all starts in your posture. The secondary angle and forward bend from your hips are the angles around which your body rotates. The secondary angle becomes a great checkpoint. The shoulders should turn around the spine, avoiding any raising up or tilting down.

Weight shift is also an integral part of the pivot. There should be more weight on the right side in the backswing and more weight on the left in the forwardswing and finish. Because the body is turning and the arms are swinging on plane, weight shift is only one piece of the puzzle. When players incorrectly shift their weight, there are two common mistakes. First is a **"reverse pivot,"** (below) which we discussed earlier. Second, players may try to get their weight too much on the left side and will end up making excessive upper body movement to the right, resulting in their head being past their right foot. This movement is called a "sway."

In a reverse pivot, the weight shifts to the left side on the backswing (above) and to the right side on the follow-through (below). This is a major swing flaw for many players.

5. Swinging the Club and Rhythm

We've talked about rhythm in putting, and it is just as critical in pitching. Counting 'tick-tock' is a very effective drill to create good rhythm throughout your game. The reason we spend some time on this subject is because it isn't as easy as it sounds. We mentioned golf's deadly instincts earlier, and they rear their ugly head to create quick, tension-filled swings. Smooth, rhythmic swings are the goal. Another way to practice this is to count "one thousand one, one thousand two" as you swing.

It is important to remember to let the laws of physics work for your golf swing. Swinging more rhythmically and multiplying your speed is only going to help you hit the ball more consistently.

6. Plane and Swing Arc

Swing plane has been misunderstood over the years, but one of the key things to understand is the circle. When you take a club and swing as if the ball is teed up at your waist, you will see a horizontal circle. We start to lower the spot where the imaginary ball is and the circle starts to tilt over until we get to ground level. We now have a good feel and outline of a basic swing plane.

The golf club is built with an angle between the clubface and the shaft. It is not built like a croquet mallet or a pool cue, which would go straight back and straight through. The angle that is created means the club is most efficiently moved along a specific shape. The shape of the swing is what is known as swing plane. Swing plane is a tremendous concept that, once pictured in your mind, shapes the way you swing and gives you an understanding of path.

"Straight back and straight through" is a misconception that leads to vertical backswings and out-to-in forwardswings. "Take the club inside" has led to swings that are too flat on the backswing and out-to-in on the forwardswing. An overall picture of the shape and some key checkpoints are what will help you develop an on-plane swing.

7. Width

Over the years, golfers have been told "Keep your left arm straight." This thought has been taken to mean stiffness in the arm. The distance from the buttons on your shirt to the butt end of the club should be maintained throughout the golf swing. This distance is the width in your swing and, just like the spokes on a wheel, it should stay consistent throughout the swing.

Improvement begins with a golfer's concept of what he or she should do to have the best game. We have identified golf's major misconceptions and replaced them with the Seven Pitching Essentials that all golfers should know. Now we will show you some drills that will make these concepts second nature. In addition to developing your ability to pitch the golf ball, you are also going to be making your full swing better. The full-swing is simply a "glorified pitch." If you are able to perfect the pitch, this will help your full swing tremendously.

Now that you are hitting the ball solidly, we need to examine what determines how far the golf ball will go. The next chapter will help you with distance control.

In the pages that follow, we've referenced the applicable pitching essential with each drill.

Pitching:
Drills

1) Line Drill

(Essential 3)

Draw a line on the ground with paint or use two tees to create an imaginary line. Make swings and take a small divot on or past that line. When you can accomplish this consistently, you will be able to hit more solid shots. If you are unable to brush the grass on that line, it is most likely because you are either falling back or bending your wrists, both of which are results of trying to "lift" the ball. Until you can consistently accomplish this task, you will not be able to move onto distance control successfully.

2) Impact Bag

(Essentials 2, 3)
Golf's best all around training aid. Pop the impact bag and you will see the hands lead and face square. Get the feeling that the bag "jumps" away from the clubface. Give the bag a healthy "pop".

3) Pivot Drill

(Essential 4)
Look in a mirror and check your set-up
(keys for set-up are earlier in the chapter).
a. While looking face-on into the mirror,
maintain the slight spine tilt as you turn.
b. While looking at the side view, make
your turn with your shoulders maintaining
a 90-degree angle relative to your spine
bent forward.

4) Circle Tilted Over

(Essential 6) Take your sand wedge and start out swinging as if the ball is teed up at your waist. This will result in a circular swing that is horizontal like a merry-go-round. Next, lower the circle as if the ball is teed up at your knees. This will result in your circle tilting over on more of a diagonal plane. Now go to ground level and make your circular swing. This creates an attitude of a whole motion instead of so many parts and a great swing plane.

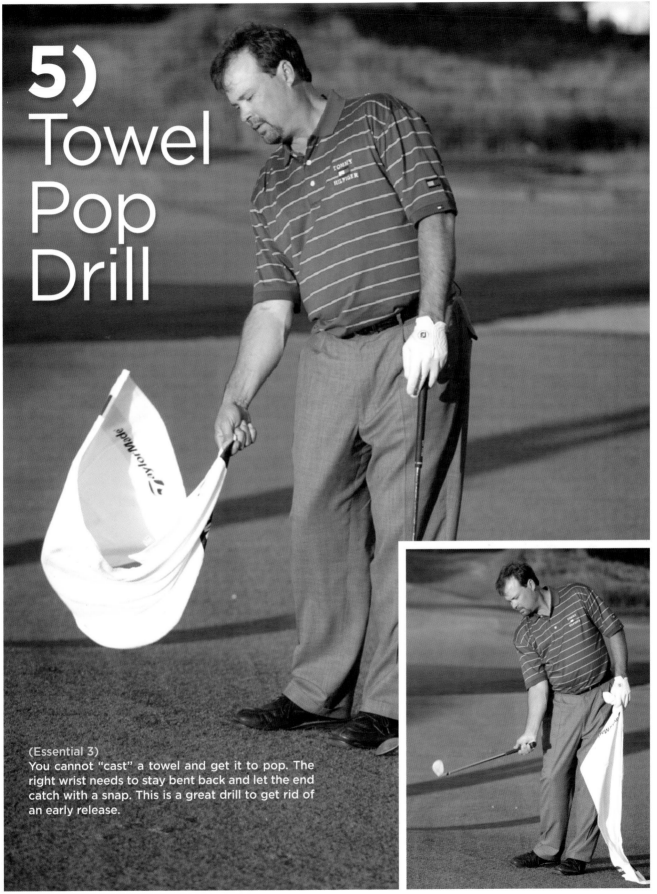

5) Towel Pop Drill

(Essential 3)
You cannot "cast" a towel and get it to pop. The right wrist needs to stay bent back and let the end catch with a snap. This is a great drill to get rid of an early release.

6) Folded Right Elbow to Folded Left Elbow

(Essentials 6, 7)
Fold the right elbow on the backswing and fold the left elbow on the follow-through. This is the simplest way to swing the club. If you are able to do this, you will have a solid foundation with which to work.

7a) Lag Drill

On this drill you will have a late hinge going back to give you the feel of lagging the wrist coming down. Another drill to get rid of an early release.

7b) Hinge & Lag Drill

In this drill you have more of a conventional pitch backswing with a 90 degree hinge and take the feel from the previous drill to lag on the way down and solid impact.

7c) Hinge to Rehinge

Make a half-swing, focusing on the hinging and rehinging of the wrists. This will allow you to create maximum clubhead speed with minimal effort.

8) Three Finger Curl Down

The three-finger curl down is a great drill if you are scooping or slicing—or both. This drill counteracts the upward tendency of a Scooper and creates the downward hit of a Striker. Take a club halfway back and then start the club down while feeling the last three fingers of the left hand "curl down." As you curl the last three fingers down, the left wrist also arches out. This is what the late Claude Harmon used to refer to as "Bethlehem Steel" at impact. "You want to have Bethlehem steel at impact son, no linguine," Mr. Harmon would exhort. Do this drill as part of your 5 minutes to Better Golf™ and you will be on the road to solid, straight shots.

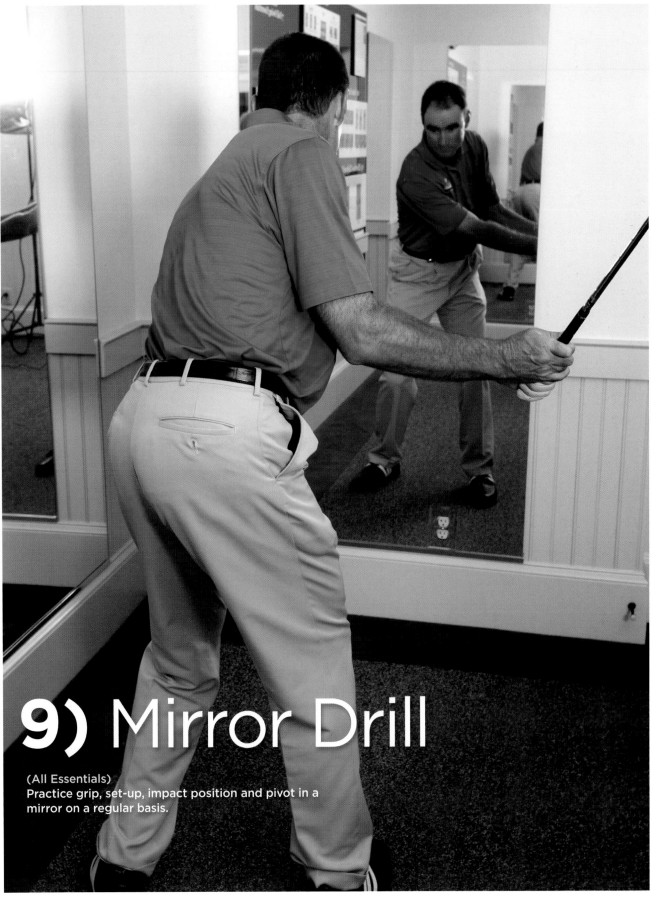

9) Mirror Drill

(All Essentials)
Practice grip, set-up, impact position and pivot in a
mirror on a regular basis.

The Chunk-and-Roll and the Flop

BELIEVE IT OR NOT, YOU'RE NOT GOING TO HIT EVERY GREEN IN REGULATION. YOU'RE GOING TO NEED CREATIVITY IN YOUR ARSENAL TO GET UP-AND-DOWN FOR PAR, OR HOLE THE OCCASIONAL PITCH FOR A BIRDIE. AROUND THE GREEN THERE ARE TWO DIFFERENT SHOTS I THINK YOU NEED TO LEARN.

The Chunk-and-Roll

Plenty of green, good lie—the chunk-and-roll is your best option.

One is called a chunk-and-roll. Play the ball back in your stance, keep your weight and hands forward, keep your left hand firm, and catch the ball on the way down. The ball will come out hot and roll a long way, and if you have a lot of green to work with, it can be a very effective shot.

The other shot is what many people call a flop shot. It's more like a bunker shot and can be very effective when you're greenside with a grassy, fluffy lie. At address, keep the ball forward in your stance. You're basically trying to slide the club underneath the ball to get it airborne. Take a full swing, with a shallow angle of descent. This takes a lot of practice, but if the grass is thick around the green, it may be your only option.

The Flop

Fluffy greenside lie, not as much green—try the flop.

"How" to Practice Pitching

1. 5 Minutes to Better Golf™ exercises to do at home:
   a. Mirror Drill practicing grip, posture and pivot in the mirror.
   b. Practice the three-finger curl down drill described earlier.
   c. Circle tilted over and swing plane work in a mirror to perfect your arc for pitching.
   d. Make small "swings" and count tick-tock to yourself to establish great rhythm.
2. Outdoor should be plenty of Line Drill work. Also, pick your favorites from our list.
3. Test yourself in this category every 4 weeks

Putting It All Together

The full swing is simply a "glorified pitch."
If you perfect the pitch, you're on your way to perfecting the full swing.

Recommended Drills Prioritized for:

PROGRAM		
Silver	1. Line Drill 2. Impact Bag	3. Pivot Drill 4. Mirror Drill
Gold *All the above plus*	1. Circle Tilted Over 2. Towel Pop Drill	3. Folded Right Elbow to Folded Left Elbow 4. Lag Drill
Platinum *All the above plus*	1. Hinge to Rehinge Drill 2. Hinge and Lag Drill	

RED ZONE SUCCESS STORIES

Carroll Clark

"Although I never played on the PGA Tour as I thought I would after my first par, golf has become a big part of my daily life."

CARROLL PLAYED GOLF FOR the first time in the fall of 1991 after returning from a Marine unit in Operation Desert Storm. He was 24 years old and not sure what his next step in life was. Over the next couple of years, he got a bug for golf in a big way and decided to make it a career.

He first met Charlie King in August of 1993 at the Golf Academy of the South in Casselberry, Florida. He entered the academy in the fall semester with a 17 handicap. And with the help of Charlie and the staff, he graduated in December of 1994 with a 5 handicap. He and Charlie set quantifiable goals that were monitored closely. "Charlie was different from other teachers I had taken lessons from in the past. We set goals and developed a plan. Charlie promised if I followed the plan my short game handicap would go down and their for my scores would go down. He was right in both circumstances."

For 12 weeks during his first semester he followed this routine.

Monday and Wednesday – Chipping and Putting

He putted 100 putts on Mondays and Wednesdays from three feet between two 2x4, he also putted 10 balls from 10, 20, 30, 40 and 50 feet to develop feel for distance. "I remember Charlie stating that most three putts are caused by a poor first putt, not a poor second putt." He chipped 25 balls to a short flag, 25 balls to a medium flag, 25 balls to a long flag and 25 balls to alternating flags for feel.

Tuesday and Thursday – Pitching and Bunker Play

He pitched 10 balls from 20, 40, 60, 80, and 100 yards to towels he laid out on the range. Carroll also used this time to worked on his alignment with two clubs laid down and used his pre-shot routine for each shot. He also went into the bunker and hit fifty balls from different lies.

His short game handicap went from 21 down to 4 in 12 weeks. Through Charlie and the staff's teaching techniques and Carroll's hard work, he had totally changed his short game and his self-confidence in his game from 100 yards and in.

"Now 11 years later I teach these short game skills to my students and I see the difference every day. One of my junior students Tyler Smith just won the National Drive, Chip and Putt in his age division. Although I never played on the PGA Tour as I thought I would after my first par, golf has become a big part of my daily life. I am now a PGA Member, Division I College Golf Coach and Director of the Tennessee PGA Junior Golf Academy. I run an Elite Junior Camp with Rob Akins each summer and introduced Rob and Charlie. These two together spend every working moment figuring out ways to simplify golf and motivate golfers. Take the Red Zone Challenge. You'll be glad you did."

7

WEDGES
DISTANCE CONTROL
FROM 30 – 100 YARDS

I HAD A LESSON

with top teacher Craig Shankland in 1991. "Golfers in the '50s and '60s were more accurate than golfers today," he told me. I said, "Come on, Craig, you're just partial to the era you came up in." Craig shot back (in his distinctive English accent): "No, Charlie. I'll tell you why golfers were more accurate then. We hit to living, breathing targets called caddies. At each Tour event there was a field designated for practice and the player's caddy shagged balls for his player."

I said, "Craig, I know that. But how do you think that led to more accuracy?"

Craig replied, "There were no sloppy shots. It was a source of pride that your caddy moved very little. Hogan's caddy would catch one-hoppers all day. Palmer's caddy might take a step. When I first got on Tour, my caddy was sprinting to catch up with the balls I was hitting." Craig then mimicked his unfortunate caddy running from side to side while watching for the ball like a baseball outfielder.

"Because of the embarrassment and because we all wanted to be like Hogan, Nicklaus and Palmer, we focused in on the badge of honor of one-hopping all of our golf balls to our caddies. This natural laser beam focus made us better."

Later in the chapter we outline a drill that came from this story, the "Happy Caddy" game. The laser beam focus of hitting to definite targets is a big factor in becoming good in this part of your game.

- Charlie King

The ball-striking principles we touched on in the last chapter are especially useful with a wedge in your hand. And when we talk wedges, we're talking distance control above all else.

> The laser beam focus of hitting to definite targets is a big factor in becoming good in this part of your game.

Studies have shown that getting up and down in the 30- to 100-yard range has the biggest correlation to your score and overall success. There are several reasons this is true. To hit it close enough to get up and down, you have be a good ball-striker, and to make the putts you need to make, you obviously have to be a good putter.

There are a couple of ways to approach wedges, and both can be successful. We recognize that each golfer is unique, and not everyone will do things the same way. Some players perform better with a more structured approach, and for you we are going to give you a definitive system. For the more feel-oriented players, we are going to talk about how to practice and think to become more consistent in your distance control.

The Structured Approach

You are a structured golfer if you tend to analyze things a little bit more deeply, and if having a system sounds like a good idea. (If you don't know whether or not you're a structured player, give this approach a try first, and you'll find out.) For you we are going to recommend controlling the length and speed of your swing to control your distance.

Here's something that's perfect for the structured golfer: the Clock Image System. Picture your swing from face on as a clock, with six o'clock at your feet and 12 o'clock at your head, with your left arm as the hands of the clock. When we talk about a 9 o'clock position, for example, we are talking about the left arm position, not the club position.

Another way to think of this: In the body parts system, you use the knees, hips and shoulders as your reference point. An example would be a hip high backswing to a shoulder high follow through to hit a 60-yard shot.

Drill — Take a sand wedge and set up a couple of targets where you know the distance (i.e. 25 and 50 yards). Hit ten shots with a 9 o'clock backswing and a follow-through to 2 or 3 o'clock. Notice where the ball lands when hit solidly. This becomes your baseline distance.

Most golfers go out onto the course totally guessing, but you can go out there with confidence in certain distances. For example, standing over a 50-yard shot and knowing it is your 9 o'clock swing will make a huge difference in your results.

As you start to master the 9 o'clock swing, do a 10 o'clock swing for a longer distance and an 8 o'clock swing for a shorter distance.

The next part of the equation is the speed you use within the length of swing. A long swing with slow speed can produce a high, soft shot. The 9 o'clock swing can hit it various distances with slow, medium or maximum speed. Generally we want you to use the medium speed as your normal speed.

What the pros do, and what you should do, is to change the rhythm of the swing to match the shortened backswing on a partial wedge shot. For a pro, each backswing takes the same amount of time, whether it's a 30-yard pitch with a short backswing, or a 60-yard pitch with a longer backswing. In other words, a pro takes the club back more slowly on a shorter swing. It takes the same amount of time to execute a half-backswing as it does a three-quarter backswing.

Several studies have shown that with most professional players, the backswing takes three times longer than from the top of the swing to impact, no matter the length of the shot. It's the same thing on a pitch shot. If you want to accelerate properly through the shot, take the club back slowly, and then it's easier to accelerate. Good rhythm is the key.

9 o'clock
backswing

8 o'clock
backswing

3 o'clock
follow through

The Inner Metronome

As we mentioned for pitching in the last chapter, we want you to continue to count to yourself as you swing. Saying "tick, tock" evenly or "thousand-one, thousand-two" promotes a rhythmic swing that stands up under pressure and gives you consistent results.

With a lot of practice, this will become natural for you, and you'll see a huge improvement in your partial wedges. And that masterful touch you see from the Tour players, that touch that seems so natural, will be yours.

Real World Example

Jim figures out his 9 o'clock swing with a sand wedge is 55 yards. The same swing with his pitching wedge goes 70 yards. With his 60-degree wedge the ball goes 40 yards. One swing, three different clubs and some of the most common distances covered. He does the some thing with a 10 o'clock swing and an 8 o'clock swing. He's got all his key distances covered.

What he finds over time is that he has so much confidence in his sand wedge, he uses it by modifying the speed of his swing off of his baseline distance. For a 40-yard shot he does his 9 o'clock swing with a slower speed. Jim has created his own system, but it all started by knowing his 9 o'clock swing distance with a sand wedge.

The Feel Approach

We hear a lot of golfers say they can do it well by feel. They just look at it and somehow they know how far to hit it. The only problem is that many times, their test scores don't bear it out. We will not allow someone to say they are a feel player. They have to prove it to us during a Red Zone test. Once we feel certain that we have a golfer who can just see it, feel it, and do it, we practice hitting to targets to sharpen their sense of feel.

It makes sense that you could be successful this way because we can toss a ball to a target 20 feet away or 40 feet away without knowing exactly how far to swing club back and through. You simply react to your target based on practice.

How to Practice for the Feel Player

We challenge this golfer and get them to challenge themselves. Not only do we pick targets, but we also create situations (imaginary bunkers, water hazards and the like on the range). We want to see if there is a situation that the golfer can conquer in a different way if necessary. The feel golfer needs to pick very specific targets and see how close they can get it to these targets.

Putting It All Together

"How" to Practice Distance Wedges

1. When you feel like you have made a habit of hitting the ball solidly, you want to start to focus on your system of touch or do it by feel.
2. Set up a target at a known distance. Hit 10 shots at a time to that target to see if there is a pattern.
3. Monitor your rhythm constantly—it is critical to Red Zone success.

Distance Wedges
Fill in the gaps

I'M GOING TO SAY SOMETHING RADICAL. IF YOU'RE PLAYING A BALL THAT IS MARKETED AS BEING FOR DISTANCE, THEN YOU'RE GIVING UP FOUR TO SIX SHOTS PER ROUND. THE REASON? THE EQUIPMENT YOU'RE USING IS MORE THAN LIKELY A POOR MATCH FOR THE BALL YOU'RE STRIKING.

If you're not paying attention to the lofts of your clubs, you're asking for trouble. Many of today's pitching wedges are lofted at 45 degrees—that's yesteryear's 8-iron. Today's gap wedge is yesterday's pitching wedge.

Let me put it this way. You amateur players rely heavily on your shorter clubs to save strokes. Say you hit a poor drive on a par 4 and have to punch it into the fairway. You're left with a 115-yard third shot into the green, and you need to get it within six feet to have a good shot at saving par.

Well, you're hitting a distance ball that's tough to control with a club that is lofted differently from what the shot calls for. It's a recipe for failure.

In other words, there's a gap in your equipment where you can least afford it. Tour players know this; that's why they carry a bunch of wedges that cover them in these situations. They understand the delicate balance between distance and control. If that's true for the pros, then it's doubly true for you amateur players. If you're like many amateurs and only hit five or six greens in regulation per round, then it's critical to carry the right wedges with the right lofts, and to play a ball that responds on the greens.

A craftsman is only as good as his tools. Make sure you're using the right lofts on your approach shots and a ball that will respond on the green.

The Happy Caddy Game

For this one you need a partner. This game came from the story at the beginning of the chapter from top teacher Craig Shankland. It dawned on me that this could be used as a practice principle, and you can use it, too. Find a partner and play the 'Happy Caddy' Game. You get to use one ball. One player stays in place while the other moves to different distances as you hit the ball back and forth to each other. When the ball is one-hopped to your partner, he is the 'Happy Caddy.' When you chunk it short or skull it long and your caddy has to run to get it, he is unhappy. This way of practicing creates focus like no other.

8

BUNKERS
THE "THUMP" VS. THE "THUD"
THE SECRETS TO GREAT BUNKER PLAY

JULIUS BOROS WAS A GREAT

champion, but he had to overcome his fear to earn his greatest victory. Specifically, it was his fear of bunkers that held him back at the 1962 U.S. Open. That fear kept him from aiming at flags and hitting it close.

Boros proceeded to spend a year on the beach, as it were. For the next year, he spent part of every day working on his sand play. Gradually, he became comfortable with his bunker shots and got the point where he truly excelled in the sand.

By the time the 1963 U.S. Open rolled around, Boros' bunker-phobia had evaporated. He was able to go after flags fearlessly. He went on to win the 1963 Open in a playoff with Arnold Palmer and Jacky Cupit, and he credited his year of bunker practice with giving him the necessary confidence.

Want to know the ironic thing? That weekend, he didn't hit his ball into a single bunker. It's not so surprising, really. Once he conquered his fear of bunkers, his swing was more aggressive and confident and he hit every green.

- Rob Akins

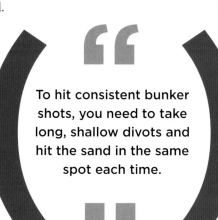

To hit consistent bunker shots, you need to take long, shallow divots and hit the sand in the same spot each time.

Today's the day you conquer your fear of bunkers.

Many PGA Tour pros will tell you in their magazine and TV tips that the bunker shot is the easiest in golf. This is pretty demoralizing when you are having difficulty even getting the ball out of the bunker, much less near the hole.

Well, guess what? Those pros are wrong. Our short game skill testing data has shown us that the bunker shot is the hardest shot in golf for most amateurs.

Rather than let that fact defeat you, we challenge you to make it a positive. Because of the initial high scores that you're likely to post in your Red Zone skills test, bunker play has the potential for the most noticeable improvement of any shot in your Red Zone arsenal.

So, what do these touring professionals know that makes the bunker shot so easy for them? You're about to find out.

The sand wedge is designed differently than any other club in your bag, thanks to Gene Sarazen, who got an inspiration while watching millionaire Howard Hughes work the controls of his airplane. "I was trying to make myself a club that would drive the ball up as I drove the club down," Sarazen said. "When a pilot wants to take off, he doesn't raise the tail of his plane, he lowers it. Accordingly, I was lowering the tail of my niblick to produce a club whose face would come up from the sand as the sole made contact with the sand." This idea led him to put solder on the back of a niblick (which was like our 9-iron) so it would skid through the sand instead of dig. He tried many different combinations until he found one he liked. He is given credit with inventing the first true sand wedge in 1931.

The 'bounce' of a sand wedge is what allowed us to start playing the shot differently. Before the sand wedge came along, the player could try to chip it out or hit it fat with a big swing. Hitting under it on purpose is what we do today, but it was not reliable because the club would dig in the sand instead of skid.

That's the genius of the sand wedge. The bottom of the club, known as bounce, is lower than the leading edge. This allows the club to skid through the sand and not dig too deep.

I know that sounds simple, but it can make a profound difference in your bunker play.

The Bunker Essentials™

In the bunker, it's easy to get sidetracked by things that are not essential. You've heard it before: Line up left, swing left, open the face and hit two inches behind the ball. Though there is truth in each of these statements, they take you away from the essential task in the bunker: Take a long, shallow divot in the bunker with the ball in the middle of that divot.

You should open the face slightly to create more 'skid' or 'bounce.' But we want you to line up parallel for the time being until the ball goes right of the target consistently. Then, and only then, should you line up to the left of the target. By focusing your attention on the most critical thing — the long, shallow divot — you will be able to master and understand bunker play thoroughly.

The reason we don't like the thought "Hit two inches behind it" is because you can accomplish that task and still go too deep and not get the ball out of the bunker. When you take that eight or nine inch shallow divot with ball in the middle of that divot, the ball flight is high and soft every time.

When practicing, all the divots you take in the sand should begin at the same place. You will need to become consistent in doing this just as you have become consistent in taking a divot at the same spot when hitting out of the fairway.

Find a practice bunker and take a few swings, knocking some sand out of the bunker. Notice how far the sand flies, where the divot starts and the sound of the club hitting the sand. Was the divot long and shallow? Are your divots starting behind the center of your stance? Does the contact with the sand sound like a pleasing "thump" or a jarring "thud"? (A "thump" would be the good one).

Once you are controlling your divots of sand, place a ball slightly ahead of the middle of your stance. Stay focused on the divot of sand as if the ball is a large speck of sand. Make the same swing, taking the long, shallow divot of sand, which will explode the ball onto the green. **Your success will be contingent on your ability to take the same long, shallow divot and start the divot in the same place.**

Thinking of it this way, distance control is relatively easy. Make the sand fly short, medium and long distances to hit short, medium and long bunker shots. You can control the distance with the length and speed of your swing.

Putting these ideas into practice will change your success in the bunker. Maybe you will be able to say it's the easiest shot in golf.

Keys and Drills
There are several keys and drills that we follow in order to help you become a more consistent player. Keep reading.

1) Set up

a) Set up a little lower. Dig your feet in to get a solid base. Your swing will now end up going down into the sand.
b) Ball positioned just in front of middle
c) Weight center to slightly left

2) Bunker Boards

Use "bunker boards" to get a sense of the club skidding through the sand. Early success with this will eliminate the fear of the bunker shot. Place a 1"x6" board in the sand. Put a scoop of sand on top of the board with a ball on top of the sand. Knock sand off the board, and watch the ball "explode" out.

3) Line Drill

This line drill is a little different than the one we used for pitching. Draw a line in the sand. If the long, shallow divot is roughly eight inches long, half of if should be before the line and half of it after the line. Practice hitting bunker shots without the ball to consistently hit the same spot and to develop a feel for the explosion effect of the sand.

To help you practice taking a consistent divot of sand, draw lines around your divot for guidance. You should develop the same long, shallow divot that starts and ends in the same place each time.

Use the length and speed of your swing to control the length of your bunker shot.

4) Take a Divot and Watch the Sand Fly

Taking a long, shallow divot and watching the sand fly onto the lip of the bunker gives you a sense of how the club propels sand and, therefore, the ball. Remember: Make sure the divot is long and shallow and is right between your feet.

5) Check the Texture of the Sand

When we set our stance in the bunker by wriggling our feet in the sand, we get a feel for the texture. When the face of the club is pointed slightly to the right (open), the flange, or bounce, increases, which keeps the club from digging even more. However, if you are in hard or wet sand, an open face will cause the club to bounce into the ball, resulting in a poor shot. So, instead of thinking that the club should automatically be opened on every shot, it is actually based on the texture of the sand.

Trouble Bunker Shots

Buried Lies, Footprints, Fried Eggs, etc.

There are several keys that need to be considered when playing a bunker shot with a buried lie. First, the club needs to dig instead of skid when hitting the ball. You need to close the clubface slightly and make a more up and down swing. In addition to this, you should not have a very big follow-through. Finally, the ball will come out because of the explosion of sand with very little spin—therefore, the ball will roll much further than a good lie bunker shot. Check the photo sequence below to see how this is done.

Distance Control

The Longer the Shot, the Longer the Follow-Through

After 20 years of study, I've decided that the best way to control distance is to control your follow-through. The longer the shot, the longer the follow-through. All the other elements of the stroke remain the same. And don't be afraid on longer bunker shots to try a different club. If you open a 9-iron, it has bounce like a sand wedge, but it will carry, release and run farther. It's a great help on the long explosion shot, which is the riskiest shot in golf.

- Rob Akins

IT'S SIMPLE.
The longer the shot, the longer the follow-through.
Continued on next page

Distance Control

Pretend as through you're tossing the sand onto the green.

RED ZONE TIP

Distance Control

For a longer toss, you'd use a longer follow-through, right?

"How" to Practice Bunker Play

1. The key here is to establish a long, shallow divot in the right place before introducing the ball.
2. When the divot is established, start to hit balls out on that same established divot. Notice if the sound stays the same. If you are doing it correctly, the ball will come out high and soft with little run. If you are hitting too far behind it, the ball will come out low and run.
3. Build confidence through success and test yourself to see how you are doing.

Don't Fear the Sand

IT'S AMAZING HOW, WHEN YOU'RE AFRAID OF SOMETHING, YOUR BALL MANAGES TO FIND IT. IT HAPPENS TO ALL OF US, WHETHER WE HAVE A FEAR OF TREES, WATER HAZARDS OR OUT-OF-BOUNDS STAKES.

Many of you no doubt have this fear of bunkers. And today's the day to overcome that fear.

In the old days, bunkers were truly hazards. They were deep, the sand was of an uneven consistency, and the equipment wasn't as specialized and effective at getting out of the sand. Today, it's a different story; pros will actually aim at bunkers to avoid the long grass by the green. You, too, can gain this level of confidence in your bunker play. Traps don't have to be as penalizing as water hazards or out-of-bounds, if you know how to play out of them.

It's a much simpler shot than most people realize. It's the only shot where hitting the big ball (the earth) before you hit the little ball is the proper play.

I want you to focus on the next challenge: distance control.

After 20 years of study, I've decided that the best way to control distance is to control your follow-through. The longer the shot, the longer the follow-through.

All the other elements of the stroke remain the same. And don't be afraid on longer bunker shots to try a different club. If you open a 9-iron, it has bounce like a sand wedge, but it will carry, release and run farther. It's a great help on the long explosion shot, which is the riskiest shot in golf.

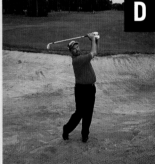

It's simple. The longer the shot, the longer the follow-through. Pretend as though you're tossing the sand onto the green. For a longer toss, you'd use a longer follow-through, right?

The "Thump" vs. the "Thud"
The Secret to Great Bunker Play

MANY PGA TOUR PROS WILL TELL YOU IN THEIR MAGAZINE AND TV TIPS THAT THE BUNKER SHOT IS THE EASIEST IN GOLF. THIS IS PRETTY DEMORALIZING WHEN YOU ARE HAVING DIFFICULTY EVEN GETTING THE BALL OUT OF THE BUNKER, MUCH LESS NEAR THE HOLE.

A: To help you practice taking a consistent divot of sand, draw lines around your divot for guidance. You should develop the same long, shallow divot that starts and ends in the same place each time. B & C: Use the length and speed of your swing to control the length of your bunker shot.

Well, guess what? Those pros are wrong. Our short game skill testing data has shown us that the bunker shot is the hardest shot in golf for most amateurs.

Now that we know that, what do we do about it? What do these touring professionals know that makes the bunker shot so easy for them? You're about to find out.

The sand wedge is designed differently than any other club in your bag. The back of the bottom of the club is lower than the leading edge. This allows the club to skid through the sand and not dig too deep. This is where the secret comes in: **To hit consistent bunker shots, you need to take long, shallow divots and hit the sand in the same spot each time.**

I know that sounds simple, but it can make a profound difference in your bunker play.

The first thing I want you to do is find a practice bunker and take some swings, knocking some sand out of the bunker. Notice how far the sand flies, where the divot starts and the sound of the club hitting the sand. Was the divot long and shallow? Are your divots starting behind of the center of your stance? Does the contact with the sand sound like a pleasing "thump" or a jarring "thud?" (A "thump" would be the good one.)

Once you are controlling your divots of sand, place a ball slightly ahead of the middle of your stance. Stay focused on the divot of sand as if the ball is a large speck of sand. Make the same swing, taking the long, shallow divot of sand, which will explode the ball onto the green. Your success will be contingent on your ability to take the same long, shallow divot and start the divot in the same place.

Thinking of it this way, distance control is relatively easy. Make the sand travel short, medium and long distances to hit short, medium and long bunker shots. You can control the distance with the length and speed of your swing.

Putting these ideas into practice will change your success in the bunker. Maybe you will be able to say it's the easiest shot in golf.

LONGER
IS BETTER

(RED ZONE TIP)

Up against the lip?
Try a longer club

The next time you find yourself under the lip with the pin on the far side of the green, don't be scared to use a longer club—a 9, 8 or even a 7-iron. Hitting a sand wedge in that situation tends to make the ball pop up in the air (right); with a longer club, the up-slope allows you to get the ball up and over the lip, and the lack of loft gets the ball moving forward (below), although you still need to open your blade to clear the lip. Remember—the longer shaft equals more power.

PERFECT 9

When you have a long bunker shot, if you use your sand wedge, it either won't get there, or you have to take too much of a chance to get it there — you might skull it, or you have to take such a big swing that you chunk it. For this shot, I want you to use a 9-iron.

With a 9-iron, when you open up the clubface, it creates effective bounce (the back edge is lower than the leading edge—see the photo at the top of this page), which lets the club skim through the sand like a sand wedge does.

So the same swing that would have gone 10 yards with a sand wedge goes 25 or 30 with a 9-iron. I don't give my students a choice—on a long bunker shot, I make them use the 9-iron.

You don't have to take my word for it. Tiger Woods used a 9-iron on the 14th hole of the PGA Championship at Medinah to hit a 50-yard bunker shot. It worked pretty well for him, didn't it?

Don't take this tip immediately to the golf course. Give yourself plenty of time to practice this shot so that you gain confidence with it.

Start with a shorter shot, then one of medium length, and finally try a long one as you get more comfortable with it.

1

2

3

4

The "Slide Under" Drill

Get a feel for the club sliding
under the ball
and through the sand

Things to Avoid:

- Hitting the ball first.
- Taking a divot that's too deep because of the fear of spinning it or skulling it.

When you're in a bunker, you're trying to hit the sand in the right way so that the sand pops the ball out of the bunker. But we're programmed to hit the ball, and nobody told us how deep a divot we should take, so we have a lot of difficulty executing what the pros call the easiest shot in golf. Swinging outside-in, like many are taught to do, doesn't help matters either. It often makes the divot too deep.

With the slide-under drill, you're looking to create a shallow divot, about eight inches in length, and you want the divot to be in the right place. Here's what you do: Take small swings, perfect the divot, and perfect the feeling of the club sliding under the ball and the ball popping up.

Once you become proficient with these small swings, the club slides under the ball easily and the handle goes left and the face of the club stays open, then you can add length of swing, and that's what gets you going toward the hole. Start small, and then build.

"
Today's the day you conquer your fear of bunkers.
— Charlie King
"

9

PRACTICE MAKES PERMANENT

I PUT IN A PHONE CALL

to Dr. Rick Jensen, a sports psychologist whom I had met several years before. "Rick, I'm putting together a program for the Golf Academy of the South and I want your input," I told him. "Fire away," he answered.

"I'm not happy with the typical paradigm of teaching where a person signs for a single lesson and hopes for a miracle. It's not like that in any other sport."

"You're right, Charlie. Golf is operating on an old way of thinking that needs to be changed," Rick said. I could hear the passion in his voice, so I knew I was onto something.

"I want to create a program that becomes the model for learning this game and creating a higher success rate," I said. "From your perspective as a motor learning guy, what are the steps to create this program?"

"The first step is to create the hierarchy of skills," Rick replied.

"That's a nice, big ten-dollar word. What's that?"

"It's you thinking about golf and deciding what's the most important skill, and then the next and the next. Once you have your hierarchy, then you start to create the program."

That conversation started a thought process that led to the program you are getting in this book today. A correct approach to setting out "how" this game is learned most effectively and efficiently. The Hierarchy of Skills that I used to create this program is in the Appendix for those who are curious to see the order I came up with.

- Charlie King

You need a plan. We all need a plan, whether it's golf, personal finances or our health. We can have it explained one hundred different ways, but if we aren't given the steps, most of us won't do it. If you follow the plan mapped out in this book on a daily basis, you will have a great chance of playing the kind of golf you are capable of.

In the past, you would get a "How-to" book or video or maybe a lesson and you would only get the "what" of learning golf. That approach teaches "fundamentals" — the grip, aim, set-up, swing plane, impact, short game, etc. This has been confusing because the premise in marketing is to be different. To differentiate ourselves as teachers, we have had decades of competition to come up

with the latest fad teaching method. It is no different than the fad diets that come and go. In order to differentiate, these methods have confused the golfer. We didn't want to fall into that trap in this book. The way we broke down the "What" in this book is by skill, in order of importance.

But what about the "How", the "How much", the "When", with "Who" or even the "Where"? These details being left out have made golf even more complicated. How could you possibly know "How," "What," "When" and "Where" to practice? What order should I learn golf? How much time should I spend per day? What type of teacher should I have help me? Doing what? Great questions and finally answered for you in the previous chapters in this book.

"This has happened in other sports and activities. Learning the piano is not a mystery. There are certain skills that are taught as you progress through your books and lessons. Learning to swim is one of my favorite analogies. If I was going to teach you to swim, I would not throw you into the deep end and say "Sink or swim." If that's how you learned to swim, though, it's doubtful that you would be effective and efficient. You would learn to dog paddle to keep your head above water and propel yourself to the side. Instead I would take you to the shallow end of the pool, get you accustomed to the water and teach you to float. You would then be shown how to kick your legs properly for efficiency and then arm motion and breathing. We would put it all together in the shallow end with your instructor nearby. When I feel like you have gained the confidence you need to swim without assistance, we would go to the deep end to show that you can swim in any depth of water."

- Charlie King

> You have the opportunity to become somewhere between good and great at a game you can enjoy for a lifetime.

This analogy has many of the elements we are looking for in golf instruction. The main one we want to point out is the identification of skills and building the learning process around those skills. Golf can be broken down in the same way by its main skills. By definition if you are becoming more skillful, you are a better golfer. Golf's version of floating is Pre-swing; grip, aim and setup. This has been modeled for you in the pictures in the Skills Chapters and you will be putting in only a few 5 Minutes to Better Golf™ exercises a day to make it into a habit. The leg kick in swimming is synonymous with Face Control and Striking the ball in pitching, chipping and putting. Controlling the face is the dominant factor in the direction of the ball and learning to Strike the ball solidly is the key to satisfying contact. Our version of the arm motion and breathing for pitching, chipping, and bunker play is Swing Plane, Rhythm, and Efficient Body Movement. Once these Skills are identified, you will do the "reps" to turn them into habits. We use reps because we all know that to build a muscle you must put your reps in. And it is an absolute certainty that your muscles will grow and get stronger if you do your repetitions correctly and with progressively more weight. It is just as certain in golf that when you do your reps for the particular Skill that you need in your game the skill becomes second nature.

You have an opportunity to become somewhere between good and great at a game that you can enjoy for a lifetime. Be willing to spend the relatively short period of time to build the habits that you need to make your golf experience second to none. Our 12 week program is designed to give simple, profound distinctions that make all the difference in the world between success and failure. You get to choose your time commitment level. We know how busy you all are. But for some of you, this is your profession, and we've set out to create a book and program whose principles are sound for all levels of golfers and can be used by all skill levels.

The Commitment Process

Follow the directions below to create a strong enough "why," a strong enough purpose. Improving in the short game is no different than losing weight or saving for retirement. These are all things we intend to do but somehow don't get around to it. The reason we maybe have not gotten around to it is we didn't go through a process to know our purpose or "why."

Many times pain leads to a strong "why". A person who has a heart attack goes on a strict diet and exercises religiously. This person has a life or death "why." Diet and exercise or else. Two things motivate us: pleasure and pain. We can get our purpose for the Challenge from the positive aspect of improving, or we can picture some of our short game failures in crucial situations to get the pain to motivate us.

Commitment Steps

1. Decide "why" you want to complete the Challenge. The more vivid the reason the better. Create a positive "why" and a negative "why." This will give you twice as much of a chance to complete the program. Example: The positive "why" could be picturing the lower scores and the ability to make pars when it matters. The negative "why" could be remembering your past failures every time you think about skipping a practice during your Challenge.

2. Write it down. Things that are written down elicit a deeper commitment and a better chance of following through.

3. Refer back to it on a regular basis, especially when you feel your commitment slipping.

Red Zone Practice Keys

1. Consistent practice is better than a long practice session every once in a while.

2. Follow the program and have trust that the improvement will take place. Be patient, especially in the early stages.

3. There are two types of practice: **technique** and **competition**. When you are improving your skills and building habits, you are working on your technique. This type of practice requires a lot of repetitions. Competitive practice is putting the ball in the hole in as few strokes as possible or beating a personal best in a category. This can be games where you compete against your personal best or where you compete against your friends. Many golfers wonder why their practice doesn't seem to translate to better scores, and a lack of competitive practice is usually why.

More Competitive Games

1) Ben Hogan Game — This is a putting game so named because of Hogan's reputation as a great ball-striker. If you hit all 18 greens in regulation, what would you shoot? Do this on a practice green. You have a birdie putt on every hole and you putt six short putts (four to six feet), six medium putts (ten to twenty feet) and six long putts (25 to 35 feet). Keep track of your personal best and compete against a friend. You can also play nine-hole games to take less time.

2) Seve Game — Seve Ballesteros was known for his imaginative short game and especially later in his career, his erratic full swing. If you missed all nine greens in regulation on your front nine, what would you shoot? At a short game area, assume you are near the green in regulation and you will get par with an up-and-down. Mix it up between chips, short pitches and bunker shots and have three easy shots, three medium shots and three hard shots. After you have hit your shot toward the hole, you can mark your putt just as you would on the course. Use your imagination to make these situations just as real as they would be on the course.

10

CHOOSING A TEACHER

What To Look for in an Instructor or Golf School

WHEN I WAS FIVE

years old, my daddy bought me a putter and a 4-wood. My backyard was the 16th hole of a municipal course in Shreveport, Louisiana. The course was at times my babysitter with afternoons spent hitting that 4-wood and putting on the green. I had pretty good hand-eye coordination and learned to hit that 4-wood without any instruction. From ages six to 11, I raced and took care of quarter horses. This takes a lot of time, so I was just dabbling at golf.

When I was 11, I got serious about golf. I practiced all the time. I took a lesson from the pro where I played. He was a respected player and he gave me great advice, "Take the Driver, 3-wood and 3-iron out of your bag. Tee off with your 5-wood or 5-iron and become the best chipper and putter in the city." I chipped and putted for hours and won the city championship in my age division for three straight years.

At 13 I decided to change my swing. After my lessons, I couldn't even hit the ball. My teacher got frustrated with me and quit teaching me. I decided to go on a quest to learn the best swing and could not find the answers in Shreveport.

By 15 I had figured a lot out by trial and error and knew I was going to be a player. The bad thing was I kept experimenting and that hurt my game. I was a good player—just not the great player I set out to be. After high school, I played in college at Louisiana Tech for a couple of years before turning pro at 21.

By the time I turned 24, after modest success I realized that I was meant to be a teacher. In this whole time I would help other players, and I got more satisfaction out of helping them then I did from my own golf game. My dream changed. I started dreaming of getting players on Tour, having them win a Tour event or a major. I liked helping people of all levels reach their goals.

I met Charlie King in 2003 and knew we wanted the same thing. We talked during a junior camp I was running in Tennessee and came up with the nuts and bolts of what became this book. We knew that even though there were thousands of books on golf, none had put together a program that a golfer could follow and get better for sure. And no book had interwoven motivation all the way through it.

I have a reputation for being tough on my players. I'll tell you something I learned a long time ago. It's not what you know that determines your success, it's what you do. I will not settle for my players being less than they can be and that now includes you.

- Rob Akins

Don't let your ego, time constraints or any other factor prevent you from getting the professional help you need to play your best golf. Even the greatest players in the world have professional instructors whom they trust. David Toms is quick to share credit for his success with his boyhood friend, teacher and co-author of this book, Rob Akins. Jack Nicklaus had a lifelong teacher in Jack Grout. Arnold Palmer's only teacher was his dad, Deacon.

Having an instructor is not a requirement for this Challenge, although it is recommended. But even choosing the right instructor can be tricky. In this chapter, we'll let you in on the inside secrets of the golf instruction industry and with this insight give you a great chance to find a teacher/coach who can take you to the next level.

Not all instructors or golf schools are created equal. If you choose an instructor or golf school to help you succeed in this program, we

> **I will not settle for players being less than they can be and that now includes you.**

want to make sure you pick the right one. In this chapter we'll go over the traits of a Master Instructor, give you a checklist for selecting a golf instructor or a golf school, and give you the eight interview questions you need to ask any prospective instructor.

One inspiration for this book was all the bad lessons we've had (the pain) and all the great instructors we've have been around (the pleasure). We want to pass on this knowledge to you so can be the passionate golfer you were when you started this game. Remember how great it felt when you first hit that perfect shot, or snaked that long putt into the hole in a crucial situation? That's what got you addicted to this game. We want to make sure you find one of these master teachers.

"For the next minute, I want you to think of the best teacher or coach you had in a class or sports. What was it about that person that makes them immediately spring to mind? Was it their dedication? Their knowledge? Their passion and enthusiasm? Did they care? I have asked this question for years in classes and seminars and the answer is much more about the subjective things as opposed to exact knowledge. Knowledge is a given. If this teacher is not knowledgeable, then you don't rank them. When I ask the people in my class or seminar to name the top attribute, I get answers like: caring, enthusiasm, sense of humor and the ability to elicit high achievement, to name a few. These attributes come from passion and dedication. The kind of passion and dedication your next instructor is going to have."

- Charlie King

Do not settle for less. Show him or her this book. Measure them against the traits of the Master Instructor, ask them the eight interview questions at right and see where they stack up. Take charge of the search process and then trust your teacher to be in charge during the lesson. You deserve the best. Period.

The Traits of a Master Golf Instructor

1. The instructor will implement a specific, organized program for improvement and not just rely on single isolated lessons. The program will include goals and a realistic time frame.
2. A short game skills test will be turned into an understandable short game handicap.
3. Your equipment will be checked to make sure you have, at the very least, the proper lie angle, shaft length and shaft flex.
4. The student will receive a set of basic stretching exercises.
5. The instructor will check for physical limitations.
6. There will be an equal emphasis on the short game and the full swing.
7. The instructor will teach the game of golf, not just the swing. This includes the mental side, course management, speed of play, rules and etiquette.
8. The instructor explains and demonstrates concepts in an understandable manner and in bite-size pieces. Information overload is not an issue.
9. The student will receive drills and/or training aids that will help turn these concepts into habits.
10. The instructor will use video analysis as a feedback tool. When used properly, video is a huge help in bridging the gap between fact and feel.
11. The instructor will convey a passion for the game of golf.

8 Interview Questions to Ask a Prospective Instructor

1. How long have you been teaching?
2. Do you teach full-swing and short game equally?
3. Are you willing to help me follow the Athlon Red Zone Challenge?
4. What do you charge and do you give a break to those who sign up for a series of lessons?
5. Could you sum up your teaching philosophy for me?
6. Do you stand behind your work with a guarantee?
7. Will you let me do a trial lesson with you to make sure we are compatible?
8. Is there a wait to get a lesson with you?

8 Interview Questions to Ask
Before Attending a Golf School

1. Do they show they care if you get better by having a follow-up program after you leave?
2. How many years of experience will the instructor assigned to you have?
3. Is this a serious golf school that is focused on making you better? Or is their belief, "People don't get better, this is just a nice vacation?"
4. What is the student to teacher ratio? (Don't settle for anything higher than four-to-one).
5. Is there at least one afternoon of an instructor on the golf course with you?
6. How many total hours of instruction will you receive, and how many of those are short game?
7. What is the teaching philosophy in 25 words or less?
8. How many rounds of golf are included?

We put this section in the book to give you some guidelines to help you make an informed choice. We hold ourselves to high standards and we want you to pick someone with high standards to help you with your game.

11

THE PSYCHOLOGY OF A GREAT SHORT GAME

TO PARAPHRASE YOGI BERRA,

90 percent of golf is half-mental. Or something like that. I think what the oh-so-wise Berra was going for was this: Controlling your nerves and your emotions is critical to success in any sport—especially golf.

If you allow one of us to be your coach, you are giving us permission to do what we know to be necessary for you to reach the outer limits of your potential. The great moments of an athlete's life are those moments, win or lose, when that person has earned the inner pride and respect of knowing they gave it their all. At that moment you have a glimpse of your life's potential. Golf mirrors life in integrity and the emotional and psychological maturity it takes to succeed. This chapter offers advanced, yet simple information on how to condition your nervous system for success in golf and life.

When I met Rob Akins, I knew there was something different about his approach to teaching golf. Rob had a weeklong summer camp for 24 junior players ranging in age from 12 to 17. A mutual friend had arranged for me to be one of the teachers for the week. I was interested in spending some time with Rob on the lesson tee, so I agreed. In that week I saw some of the most unorthodox (by golf standards) techniques of any teacher I had been around. Rob alternately yelled, whispered, provoked and massaged the ego of the junior he was working with depending on what he felt the situation called for. I mention this to you because we have all been told how mental golf is. We see advice that is typically rooted in being nice to yourself and positive. But when we are honest with ourselves, we realize that many times it was the person who was willing to tell us the truth who influenced us the most. We have to know that the person cares.

> The great moments of an athlete's life are those moments, win or lose, when that person has earned the inner pride and respect of knowing they gave it their all.

For this junior week we would stay up late preparing for the next day by reviewing each junior's swing and getting on the same page about our instruction. Rob cares enough to prepare and he cares enough to tell the truth. In this chapter I want to give you a flavor of what you would get in a lesson with Rob, along with some tried and true information that I feel I can simplify for you to conquer the mental side.

That week planted the seed that led to this book. Rob was putting together a way of measuring the short game, handicapping it and setting a program for improvement. When I told him I already had done that and we had a similar desire to give golfers 'real' information that would lead to real improvement, the Red Zone was on its way. After meeting Rob, I wanted to bring his unique brand of golf instruction and motivation to you. What follows is an interview I did with Rob about his approach to reaching his players. It is 'real' and at times raw, but I can tell you in my 16 years of teaching, I haven't seen anyone motivate the way Rob does. The information in this book tied with this chapter on our motivation techniques will give you a complete idea of how to take your game to the next level.

- Charlie King

Rob Akins on Psychology

Warning: Don't Read This Section Unless You Can Handle the Truth

Charlie King sat down with Rob Akins and captured Rob's thoughts on motivation, mental toughness and what is required to develop a proper mindset for golf. Rob's comments are recorded below.

On how he's different from other teachers:

I don't look at their golf swings first. I ask questions and I look into their eyes to see what they are afraid of. Fear is at the root of our mental struggles on the golf course. You've got to understand what you are afraid of. To improve on the golf course you must practice to make skills better and you MUST face your fear. This is at the heart of whether you can take your changes from the range to the course.

I apply pressure during most lessons. I need to know what you can take and what you can't. My players are mentally tough in tournaments because I simulate tournament pressure. If you get rattled by other players, I become that other player. I use gamesmanship as you swing or putt. If you're afraid of hitting in the water, I take you to a pond or lake and we knock a few in on purpose. Hell, it's no big deal. You're still alive. It's just golf. Play the game. Compete.

Put Yourself in the Game

I want to tell you a story that is one of my favorites.

In 1958, a young sophomore football player began the season as the third-string quarterback. It looked like he would have to wait his turn. In the opening game against Texas, Georgia was losing in the third quarter, 7–0, and the offense had stalled again. While the coach watched, frustrated, from the sideline, the young man walked over to him and pleaded, "Let me go in. I can move the team."

The coach didn't say a thing. Then Georgia regained possession, and this time the young quarterback did not ask to play again. He just ran onto the field, pretending not to hear the coach yelling at him to get off the field. It was too late for the coach to stop him. Fran Tarkenton went on to move Georgia 95 yards to a touchdown. After the two-point conversion, his team led 8–7.

I'm not sure if we would have known who Fran Tarkenton was if he had not been bold enough to put himself in the game. He was too small, and his college coach didn't think he would make it in the pros. How many limitations do people tell you that you have? Are you ready to overcome any perceived weaknesses? Fran Tarkenton boldly put himself into the game and I want you to do the same thing in golf: Put Yourself in the Game.

During a Lesson, I'm in Charge

One time a very successful multi-millionaire flew in from the West Coast to see me . I was running behind schedule, because I don't teach by what the clock says. I teach by when we have accomplished what we set out to accomplish. This man was obviously upset and he told me, "In my business all our meetings start on time." I had to set him straight, "Listen, you flew two thousand miles to see me. I didn't fly two thousand miles to see you. This is my office and my busi-

ness. I treat every lesson the same. When we start, I see what you need and we are going to stay here until it happens. To hell with who's next in line. All of my players know this. If you have to wait, tough."

I'll say it again: The range is my office. I'm in charge. I know what's best for your golf game. If the player thinks they know more than I do, they shouldn't come to see me.

On why he's constantly booked despite his unorthodox methods:

A lot of times I'm the only one in a person's life willing to tell them the truth. Nobody likes criticism, even if it's called constructive criticism. I tell my players the truth because I care just like I care for my own kids. That's what comes across at the end of the day. Most people have been told what they want to hear for so long, they start to believe it. I've got to create a belief system that brings out the best in a player. We don't always like the truth, but we respect it.

The end result is self-esteem. I feel I have a great chance to make a difference in my players' lives. So I ask them a question, "How good are you?" I usually get a deer-in-the-headlights look from the player. People don't want to be wrong, so they say, "I don't know."

So I ask a little bit differently, "Who are you, really?" I then get various answers about "I am the son of …" or "I want to be the best player I can be."

I then tell them, "I know exactly who you are."

"Who's that?" they normally respond.

"Isn't that funny—I know who you are and you don't?"

"Okay, tell me."

"You are whatever you deeply believe you are. No more and no less."

My players usually respond with "What do you mean?" An example I give is if you believe you are a great putter, you will go to great lengths to prove it. After one bad putting day, you will consider it a fluke. After two bad showings, you will practice and check the fundamentals that made you great and maybe see your teacher. You will not stand for bad putting if you believe you're great.

Tiger is the best because he believes he's the best. The willpower he showed in 2004 to make cuts while he was struggling with his swing change is truly amazing.

How many of us have gone out and hit it good and putted bad or hit it bad and putted good and came up with the same score? There's a thermostat inside our head that finds a way to make our beliefs about ourselves true. Do we leave any doubt with our kids that they will learn to walk? Hell, no. We praise them for trying when they fall down. We do whatever it takes to help them overcome their fear of falling and hurting themselves. We are patient and we don't give up on our kids because they don't get it right the first time. How many of you have given up too quickly?

The reason we practice is to prove the belief that is being developed. You don't just think it. You start to see it. In this age-old chicken-or-the-egg question, I say it is the original belief in yourself that will get the practice to be more productive and mean something.

I'll give you an example. I go lift weights and I know that I can bench-press 200 pounds, but I've never been able to lift more than

200 pounds. Sure enough, I try to lift more and I can't do it. The next time I work out, my workout partner slips an extra 10 pounds on there to make it 210. I think I've got 200 pounds on there so I find a way to get it up. This is the power of belief. You will find a way to make your deeply-held belief come true.

Here's a story I heard that illustrates what we've been talking about. Inside all of us is a white dog and a black dog. The white dog is what is good about us—the honesty, morals and beliefs for a compelling future. The black dog is our dark side—the doubts, fears, and dark thoughts inside of us. The dog that is the strongest is the one you feed the most. Are you feeding the white dog with strong beliefs and great practice habits or are you feeding that black dog with doubts and excessive anger? The one thing I haven't told you: The black dog is stronger. He will eat the white dog if you don't feed the white dog. If you feed the white dog, the black dog will always be there, but you can keep him at bay.

Three Buckets

I believe in life we have three buckets — one large, one medium and one small. The large bucket has rocks. These rocks include your moral character, your faith, honesty, integrity and love. The medium bucket has pebbles. These pebbles include your family, friends, job and community. The small bucket has sand. The sand includes wealth, fame, recognition, jewelry and cars.

A person striving for the bucket of sand first cannot fit the pebbles and rocks in their bucket. They are destined for emptiness. A person striving for the bucket of pebbles can fit the sand but not the rocks. This person is happier but knows there is something missing. A person striving for the bucket of rocks can fit the pebbles and the sand in his bucket. This is where fulfillment comes from. This person can have it all because they started with the bucket of rocks as their foundation.

In golf, your bucket of rocks includes your identity, belief system and work ethic. Your bucket of pebbles includes your putting stroke, short game skills and golf swing fundamentals. Your bucket of sand includes birdies, pars, trophies and money. Take care of golf's rocks before you can expect the pebbles and sand to fit in the bucket.

I'm Gonna Make It

When you are standing over a four-foot putt, I want you to have one thought and say it over and over and over: "I'm gonna make it." From what I've been told, the human mind cannot think positively and negatively at the same time. If you keep that thought as you get ready to putt, you will have the certainty it takes to make a confident stroke.

A Kid's Grades

I work with a lot of junior players as well as having three sons. Grades in school are very important, and it is always an issue with a certain number of kids. When I have a junior player who is struggling with grades I will ask him or her, "What grades do you set out to get?" When the answer is "B's and C's," I know where the problem is. I tell them, "When your belief is that you are a B or C student, you will do what it takes to make B's and C's. You are happy with 80 on a test. You don't study any harder. You don't ask more questions. You don't work at it any harder. If you change what you won't stand for, your grades will change."

Guess what, golfers, it's the same for you. We develop a comfort that is an identity of who we are. We're a five handicap or a 90 shooter or a 30 handicap. We find a way to make that identity a reality. Set your target higher and do what it takes to get there.

Charlie King on Psychology
Do you control your Emotional State?

Your emotional state is the emotion that you are feeling at any given moment. Some are appropriate for your best golf and some are not. Out of control anger, frustration, depression, and resignation are emotions that hurt your performance. You know that, but have you learned what to do about it? My research on this subject has taken me to many experts, books and seminars. The information I present here has been primarily influenced by peak performance coach Tony Robbins and my good friend, performance expert Dr. Rick Jensen.

How do you control your emotional state while playing golf? There are three primary factors: 1) Your physiology. 2) What you are focused on. 3) The language you are using internally and externally.

Your physiology is how your body moves and your posture. Are you erect and confident or are you slumped and down? How are you breathing? Full, deep breaths or shallow breaths? What do your eyes show? Fear, anger, concern? Or confidence? The question becomes, "Am I in control of my physiology or do I let my circumstances dictate it?" Until we take conscious control of our body, we are at the whim of circumstance and having control is as simple as deciding. Think of a time when you were playing your best golf. Picture how you walked, stood, spoke. Can you do this consciously or do you have to wait for good golf to give you this physiology and feeling?

What you focus on and how you focus are critical to your peak golf state. If you picture a ball flying majestically toward the flag and landing within inches of the hole, you will have a completely different internal experience than if you entertain the thought even for an instant of the ball curving toward the water. Your brain will take the picture and trigger the emotion that is associated with that experience. You can also control your focus with brightness, color and sound, to name a few.

The language you use determines where your emotions are and where they are headed. Weak tone of voice, whiny voice, and weak words can take you in an unhelpful direction. Weak, impotent words lead to weak, impotent emotions and actions. Strong words like "I will ...", " I MUST ...", "Let's go ..." lead to a state of certainty and confidence.

Why is your emotional state important? Can you imagine Tiger Woods saying to himself, "I hope I pull this shot off" or "I wish I had better luck"? Can you imagine Michael Jordan walking into a game slumped and meek? Or Mike Tyson in his prime looking frightened? Or Jack Nicklaus saying, "I might be able to beat these guys?" Of course not. These great athletes were confident and unstoppable. They didn't show up looking for second place and their body and language showed it. In his prime, Larry Bird would show up for the 3-Point Shootout at All-Star weekend and ask his competitors, "Which one of you guys is coming in second?" That's confidence.

Do you have to wait for good results to be confident? Absolutely not. You will see better results in our 12-week challenge if you decide in advance to go through it in a confident, unstoppable mental state. It's logical to proceed this way. Your body is responding to the signals from the brain and vice versa. You are learning new movements and integrating them. If you approach it with a sense that you have already achieved it, then your brain will be picturing good shots, better scores and the satisfaction that goes with them. If you approach the process with trepidation, your brain is picturing the "What if's".

What if this doesn't work? What if I'm just not good enough? What if I try and fail? These what-if questions lead to pictures in the brain, which lead to emotions. None of these emotions help the process. The process of controlling your emotional state through your physiology, focus and language not only helps your golf game, but are the same mechanics that we all should have been taught to have a more rewarding life.

Here are your daily assignments that will transform your emotional state to one of strength and confidence.

1) Control your Physiology — Stand tall with your chest up and your center of gravity strong. Plant your feet solidly at shoulder width. Focus on your navel and feel your ab muscles go one inch in and 2 inches up. Be like a linebacker who can't be moved. Feel strong and unstoppable. Imagine how Tiger looks and feels when he heads to the first tee and everyone can see from his posture and demeanor that he is the man to beat. Decide in advance that you are not only going to play golf this way, but also live life this way. This is a conscious commitment.

2) Practice the Ability to Choose Your Focus — Whatever you focus on will determine how you feel at any given moment. Why do some people cry at a sad movie? After all, you don't know the characters and it is make-believe. You cry because for that moment, you decide that the situation is real. It's real to your nervous system. In golf, you can create your own movie and the corresponding feelings anytime you want to. When you feel nervous in a tournament, your brain is entertaining the thought of failure and that focus leads to fear, nervousness and tension in the body. Needless to say, that doesn't help you perform. If instead you calmly focused on executing the shot at hand, you would feel strong and confident.

3) Choose Your Words — In your daily talk, are you using strong, confident words that mirror confident performance, or are you saying weak words that mirror your self-doubt? For example, don't say 'try'. It's either do or don't. 'Might' is replaced by 'will' and 'should' is replaced by 'must'.

4) Say it Like a Drill Sergeant — Drill sergeants take raw recruits and create a different belief system during basic training. I want to change the voice inside your head for the next 12 weeks. Some of you may have a nice voice that says everything is OK, but if the voice for these 12 weeks belonged to your favorite team's coach or to a drill sergeant, you would get different results. Think about Louis Gossett, Jr. from *An Officer and a Gentleman*—pushing Richard Gere to surpass his self-imposed limits. This image, this voice is screaming at you when you think about giving up or not doing your daily practice. This voice won't let you settle for second best in your life and your golf game.

Think of this scenario. You want to do the program. It all makes sense, but you have questions and doubts start to pop up in your head. What if I don't get better? What if I try and I fail? Why put that much work into a silly game? The answers to these questions are not inspiring. Instead of these weak "What if..." questions, you hear a voice that says "Just Do It." This voice is stern and demanding. You know deep down you can accomplish a lot more than you are, but you let yourself off the hook. This coach, this voice won't let you off the hook. This voice will say, "Get it done." You fill in the blank. You know what this voice needs to say to keep you on track and motivated.

Affirmations are saying things to yourself that you want to be true in your life. The problem is we don't say it with enough emotion. All of us are talking to ourselves constantly. We have questions that we ask, answers to those questions and a tone of voice that answers those questions inside our head. Part of your success in this program is the way you handle this internal communication. Take statements that you want to become true in your life and say them with conviction and full emotion. Get your whole body involved, your facial expressions, and the tone of your voice. I find the car is a good place to do this so you can let it rip. For these 12 weeks take key statements and be your own drill sergeant for golf's basic training.

Do a Rocking Chair Test

A Rocking Chair Test is to take yourself to your 85th birthday or beyond and sit in a rocking chair thinking about your life. What are you the most proud of and what do you regret? For this exercise we are going to focus on your golf game. How much more could you have enjoyed your rounds of golf if you had made the Essentials into habits? What would 12 weeks of commitment in your life have meant for the next 15 to 50 years of improved golf? Really picture your game 50% better than it is now and playing the upcoming season. The increased pride and confidence. The ease of swinging the club. More putts falling, especially the short ones. More distance. All of this can be yours by following the 12-Week Challenge.

12

5 MINUTES TO BETTER GOLF™
ILLUSTRATED

1) Your Credit Card Can Make You Money

A

A: Find yourself a straight-on 8-foot putt. Once you think you've lined up correctly, have your buddy replace the ball with a credit card. The card will tell you the exact direction your putter face is pointing. B/C: Place the ball on top of the card, and putt.

B

C

2) The Putting Plane

By allowing the putter to follow the slightly tilted plane, you create the feel for a perfect path.

3) Right Hand Only

When putting with one hand, golfers naturally swing the putter and don't guide the ball. This leads to a sense of truly rolling the ball and not over-controlling and guiding it.

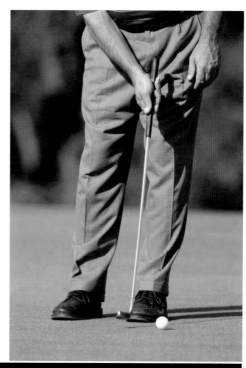

When you putt with your right hand only, it really forces you to swing the putter.

4) Look at the Hole

One of our favorites. This drill is simple. Instead of looking at the ball as you putt, look at the hole. Free-throw shooters don't focus on the ball; they look at the hoop. Like basketball and other sports where you get a good sense of the target by looking at it, the same thing happens in your putting. After the first few awkward putts, most golfers notice they develop an uncanny sense of speed and direction. Golfers have an innate sense of touch; they simply need something to draw it out of them. This drill does it.

Golfers have an innate sense of touch; they simply need something to draw it out of them. The "Look at the Hole" drill does it.

5) Putting Mat

Watching the ball go in and creating a pattern of success is the key to the putting mat. Many of these drills in this section should be adapted to the mat.

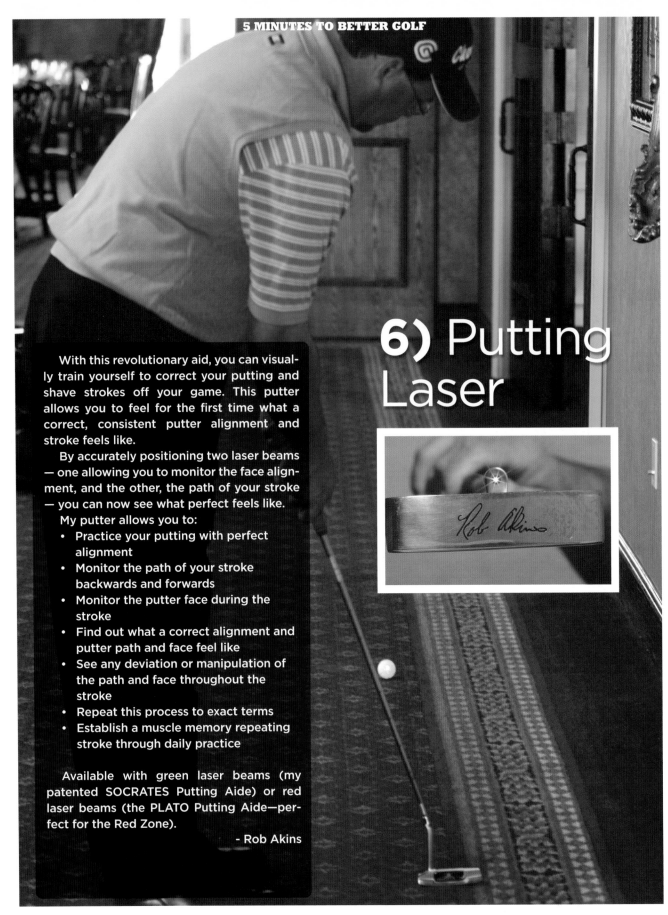

6) Putting Laser

With this revolutionary aid, you can visually train yourself to correct your putting and shave strokes off your game. This putter allows you to feel for the first time what a correct, consistent putter alignment and stroke feels like.

By accurately positioning two laser beams — one allowing you to monitor the face alignment, and the other, the path of your stroke — you can now see what perfect feels like.

My putter allows you to:

- Practice your putting with perfect alignment
- Monitor the path of your stroke backwards and forwards
- Monitor the putter face during the stroke
- Find out what a correct alignment and putter path and face feel like
- See any deviation or manipulation of the path and face throughout the stroke
- Repeat this process to exact terms
- Establish a muscle memory repeating stroke through daily practice

Available with green laser beams (my patented SOCRATES Putting Aide) or red laser beams (the PLATO Putting Aide—perfect for the Red Zone).

- Rob Akins

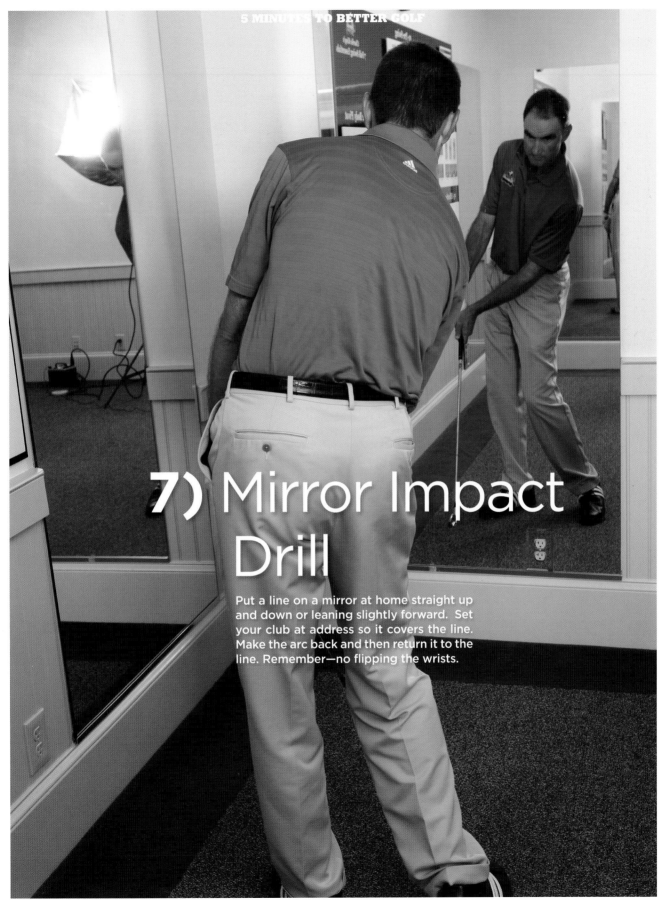

7) Mirror Impact Drill

Put a line on a mirror at home straight up and down or leaning slightly forward. Set your club at address so it covers the line. Make the arc back and then return it to the line. Remember—no flipping the wrists.

8) Ping Pong Ball

You can use this drill inside. Hit chip shots with a ping pong ball. Notice how hitting slightly down makes the ball go up and puts some spin on the ball. Be creative and take what you learn to the real ball. I have all my juniors and many of my adult players use this drill indoors. This drill teaches my players touch, the effects of spin and imagination. It also helps you develop your intuition when chipping — that's critically important. I used to chip ping pong balls onto my dining room table at home and try to get them to stay there. It's a fun, competitive little game to play with a partner, and one that really helps you learn to shape your shots. And while you've got the ping pong balls out, experiment with them. See what it takes to make them curve. Hit draws and fades. You can easily pick up little habits to take with you to the course.

-Rob Akins

9) The Punisher Club

Take the club you are chipping with, then take another club out of your bag and turn it over and hold the two clubs so the upside down club sticks out beside your left hip. When you chip the ball the goal is for the upside down club not to hit you in the side. If you scoop and the club hits you, that is your "punishment."

The Pitching Essentials™
10) The Pre-Swing

The pre-swing is made up of three key elements: GRIP, AIM, AND SET-UP.

Grip

The grip has three purposes:
1) To hinge the club
2) To square the face
3) To support the club at the top

Hinge the club

First, to correctly hinge the club, you should take the grip-end of the club and hold it only with the heel pad (which is placed on top of the grip) and the forefinger. You should then move the club up and down to check if the club is hinging properly. When you wrap your remaining three fingers around the club, you should see two or three knuckles on the left hand. If you see four knuckles, the grip is too strong; if you see no knuckles or just one knuckle, then the grip is too weak.

Next, you should place your right hand on the side of the club.

The way you put your hands on the club allows you to achieve the second function of the grip, which is to square the clubface.

Now, take the club to the top of your backswing. Your left thumb and the pad of your right forefinger should support the club. If you are doing this with your grip, you now have a correct, functional grip.

There is a misunderstanding about light grip pressure. We like to see that the pressure in the arms and wrists is light and the fingers are snug on the club. This gives us the best of both worlds: speed from light arm and wrist pressure and support of the club through snug fingers on the club.

Square the Face

Support the Club at the Top

Aim

Many players set up with their shoulders lined up to the target. This is another one of golf's misconceptions because, in reality, the player is now lined up to the right of the target. Because the clubface hits the ball, it only makes sense that you should line up your clubface with the target. A key principle to remember when going through your pre-shot routine is "clubface first, body second." Another key concept to remember is the shoulders are lined up parallel to and left of the target. The lower body should be lined up slightly left to create resistance for the backswing. This resistance creates a stopping point. Because players are standing sideways and dealing with visual distortion, it takes practice and feedback to become good at alignment.

Set-up: Posture

Why is good posture important? Because bad posture has three devastating effects: It restricts your arm movement; it restricts your body turn; and it leads to injuries.

When you stand straight, the back has a very small "s-shaped" curve. When you have good posture, the spine is healthy, and there should be a small gap between the vertebrae. Between vertebrae there is tissue called a disc, which acts as a cushion. When your posture gets slouched forward, the vertebrae touch, and the discs get squeezed and pinched. When this happens and you take your backswing, the vertebrae are grinding on each other and pinching the discs. This happens shot after shot, for years. The discs get inflamed and the back pain kicks in. Eventually you are unable to play because the pain is so severe.

So how do we avoid this? Well, one of the main principles in the set-up is to bend from the hips, not the waist. If you bend from the waist, your spine will be in the unhealthy position we just described. You must also have a slight knee flex to keep your weight balanced. This will get you in an athletic, balanced position to start your swing. We check this by giving you the "push" test. Once you take your posture, we give you a light push forward and backward to see that you are centered and cannot be pushed over easily. This allows you to learn to "feel" correct posture and weight distribution.

When you grip the club, your right hand is slightly lower than your left hand; corresponding to this, your right shoulder should be lower than your left. This slight tilt of the upper body we call "secondary angle." This secondary angle should be maintained throughout the golf swing.

Stance

Your feet should be shoulder width apart for most shots. The rule of thumb here is that a stance that is too narrow will cause you to lose balance easily, and a stance that is too wide will restrict your turn.

11) Towel Pop Drill

You cannot "cast" a towel and get it to pop. The right wrist needs to stay bent back and let the end catch with a snap. This is a great drill to get rid of an early release.

12) Pivot Drill

Look in a mirror and check your set-up (keys for set-up are earlier in the chapter).
a. While looking face-on into the mirror, maintain the slight spine tilt as you turn.
b. While looking at the side view, make your turn with your shoulders maintaining a 90-degree angle relative to your spine bent forward.

13) Circle Tilted Over

Take your Sand Wedge and start out swinging as if the ball is teed up at your waist. This will result in a circular swing that is horizontal like a merry-go-round. Next, lower the circle as if the ball is teed up at your knees. This will result in your circle tilting over on more of a diagonal plane. Now go to ground level and make your circular swing. This creates an attitude of a whole motion instead of so many parts and a great swing plane.

14) Folded Right Elbow to Folded Left Elbow

Fold the right elbow on the backswing and fold the left elbow on the follow-through. This is the simplest way to swing the club. If you are able to do this, you will have a solid foundation with which to work.

15) Three Finger Curl Down

The three-finger curl down is a great drill if you are scooping or slicing—or both. This drill counteracts the upward tendency of a Scooper and creates the downward hit of a Striker. Take a club halfway back and then start the club down while feeling the last three fingers of the left hand "curl down." As you curl the last three fingers down, the left wrist also arches out. This is what the late Claude Harmon used to refer to as "Bethlehem Steel" at impact. "You want to have Bethlehem steel at impact son, no linguine," Mr. Harmon would exhort. Do this drill as part of your 5 minutes to Better Golf™ and you will be on the road to solid, straight shots.

16) Line Drill

Draw a line on the ground with paint or use two tees to create an imaginary line. Make swings and take a small divot on or past that line. When you can accomplish this consistently, you will be able to hit more solid shots. If you are unable to brush the grass on that line, it is most likely because you are either falling back or bending your wrists, both of which are results of trying to "lift" the ball. Until you can consistently accomplish this task, you will not be able to move onto distance control successfully.

17) Hinge to Rehinge

Make a half-swing, focusing on the hinging and rehinging of the wrists. This will allow you to create maximum clubhead speed with minimal effort.

18) Impact Bag

Golf's best all around training aid. Pop the impact bag and you will see the hands lead and face square. Get the feeling that the bag "jumps" away from the clubface. Give the bag a healthy "pop".

Appendix A
RedZone Recommended Training Aids

We have assessed many training aids over the years, and our experience tells us that many times the simplest aids are the best. Below you will find the training aids that are listed in the earlier chapters of the book we have found are the simplest and the best. Consider the products listed below as your Red Zone Challenge Starter Kit. You can purchase these aids separately at www.golfaroundtheworld.com .

1. **Putting Mat -** This will allow you to practice your 5 Minutes to Better Golf™ drills inside.

2. **Stakes and Strings (or Pencils and Strings) -** This aid is one of our favorites and was listed by Tiger Woods as his favorite putting aid.

3. **The Putting Laser -** Designed by Red Zone co-author Rob Akins, this aid allows you to develop a perfect putting arc and face angle.

4. **Arc Board -** This aid is critical for developing a great path in your putting stroke. The Plexi Putting Track and the EyeLine Putting Plane are two that we recommend.

5. **Metronome -** This aid can be used throughout your game, from putter to driver, to help you develop rhythm.

6. **almostGolf™ Balls -** These are perfect for indoor chipping practice. You can also use ping-pong balls.

7. **Impact Bag -** One of the best. When you hit the bag, you develop a feel for good, solid impact.

8. **Essentials of Impact Board -** This aid is coming soon. Developed by Red Zone co-author Charlie King, this aid will allow you to practice the Line drill in your home. Check back frequently with athlonsports.com for its debut.

9. **Splash Board -** This board will help you gain confidence out of the bunker.

Appendix B
Charlie King Hierarchy of Skills

Starting with your putting grip and working your way out to the full swing is the best way to build a dependable golf game. In building your game, follow the order below; each subsequent level includes the preceding Skills:

Putting
1. Grip, Set-up
2. Clubface Angle
3. Speed
4. Centered Hits
5. Aim
6. Path
7. Swinging the Club, Rhythm

Chipping
8. Using a lofted club (Impact)

Pitching
9. Grip (3 Functions of a Grip)
10. Set-up
11. Hinging the Club
12. Width
13. Swing-Plane
14. Pivot (Body Movement)
15. Length of Swing
16. Connection, Timing

Full-Swing
17. Make same correct swing and length of shaft and loft take care of distance.

Bunker Play
18. Take a consistent divot of sand
19. Sand moves the ball
20. Mental Game and Course Management

Rob Akins' BIG THREE

/// The Face Imperative
/// The Path Imperative
/// The Lag Imperative

Whether you're putting, pitching or have the big stick in your hands, these three factors are all at work. These are the elements that are common to every facet of your game, and mastering each of them is essential to good golf.

The 3 Imperatives – **Putting**

You need to keep the clubface square to the target—the face imperative. Address the ball and hold the putter up as I'm doing in the photo, then simulate a putting stroke from this position. If the face remains vertical to the ground, then it's square to the target. As I putt, the face stays "vertical," or square. If I can keep the face "vertical," then I'm in control of this first variable. It's critically important. As I putt, the face may appear to be opening and closing, but it's not, which you'll see if you stand upright like I'm doing in the photo. If the putter head is vertical to the ground, your face is still square. Same thing on the follow-through.

As I simulate my putting stroke from this vertical, upright position, my clubhead stays in a square position relative to the target.

Being able to swing the club on plane—the path imperative.
Here, I use the shaft as my reference. At address, if I lift the club up again and simulate a swing from this position, I need to keep the shaft parallel to the ground as I swing back and through. If I do that, the club is staying on plane.

Look at the photos at right. If the putter is pointing to the target line on the way back and on the way through, it quickly becomes obvious when it's off plane. When I bend over into proper address position, using the flagstick as a reference, I can point my putter shaft at the line formed by the flagstick to get a feel for the proper plane. My putter shaft is not over the line, but it's pointed at it. I just want to make sure as I go back and forth that my putter shaft is always pointed at the target line.

In the photos above, right, I'm losing my path imperative. To get a feel for this, I can use a flagstick as a reference point (above, left).

The clubhead never gets ahead of the handle—the lag imperative. This simply means that you're never going to take the putter head and push it toward the ball—that gets the putter head ahead of the handle. Instead, the putter head follows the handle to the ball. If you violate this principle, you can affect the other two imperatives as well; the face can stray from its square position, and the club can get off path. If I swing back, and I push the putter head toward the ball, there's no way I can make solid contact. But if the handle is always leading, I've got the lag imperative down pat.

The No. 1 problem in putting, and in golf, is over-acceleration of the clubhead. The biggest flaw in a Tour player's or an amateur's game is that they're trying to strike the ball with the clubhead, so that when they swing down, their brain is trying to move the clubhead toward the ball. That's where the yips come from — from anticipating impact. You need to think like there is really no ball. You're just trying to swing the grip through, and the grip is pulling the head. You're never trying to push the head; you're always trying to push the handle. These three imperatives are significant in putting, but they're even more important chipping and pitching, and more important still on the full swing.

NO YES

In the photo above, left, I've lost my lag imperative. The clubhead needs to "lag" behind the handle, as in the photos in the middle and at right. If the putter head follows the handle to and through the ball, I've maintained my lag.

The 3 Imperatives – **Chipping and Pitching**

As we move to chipping and pitching, you want to feel the same thing as you did in putting. Your three imperatives are intact: The face is square, the swing is on plane, and the handle leads the clubhead through the ball. The shaft is still pointing at the target line as I pivot through the ball.

In chipping and pitching, the biggest mistake in terms of trying to meet the three imperatives is not using enough loft. In order to create loft, players throw away their lag imperative (below, left). They're trying to get the shaft to lean back to lift the ball in the air. This creates the skull, the chili-dip—nasty words that you need to banish from your golf vocabulary.

You've got to make sure that you're chipping with enough loft, so that you don't ever feel like you have to increase the loft artificially. You're always able to keep the lag. As we go through this, and you start trying to strike the ball harder, that impulse to move the clubhead and lose the lag imperative becomes even stronger. You've got to fight it. You're not moving the clubhead faster; you're pivoting and turning faster, keeping the lag imperative, and you're able to hit the ball farther.

NO | YES

The Pivot

The pivot becomes extremely important when we turn to chipping and pitching. You don't have to worry about the pivot when you putt, because you're not hitting it as far.

It's very important that when I chip and pitch, in order to swing through, my body has to pivot both backwards and forwards to create more energy and power. People who chip poorly have no pivot.

Again, the three imperatives come into play here. As I pivot, I keep the face square, keep the club on plane and keep my lag—so I have complete control. If I try to manipulate the clubface to hit the ball, I have to move something to do it, and that leads to inconsistency.

The chip is exactly the same as the putt; you've just added a pivot to make it a bigger swing.

The pitch is a glorified chip. I only hit a pitch shot when I need a little extra power that the chip doesn't give me. I'm going to make a bigger pivot, but I'm also going to allow myself to start hinging my wrists more as I pivot back, so that I create another lever. As I pivot forward, and my wrists un-hinge, that gives me more speed.

As I pivot, I keep the face square, keep the club on plane and keep my lag—so that I have complete control (below, left). On the other hand, if I try to manipulate the clubface to hit the ball, I have to move something to do it, and that leads to inconsistency (below, center and right).

YES | NO | NO

You can see this in the photos below, with the shaft extended in front of my face. If I chip the ball, the shaft is still pretty much in my eyes on the follow-through. But when I pitch, my head ends up above the shaft, because I need a bigger pivot. I'm always staying be-hind the shaft, but I'm not staying down.

I know you've probably heard, "Stay down, stay down, stay down." But it's impossible to pivot properly though the ball on a pitch shot without the left leg straightening and the body coming up. It's very important to know that if I pitch, my head is going to come up. I'm not trying to lift it, but the turning of my body is pulling me up. If I try to stay down, I'm going to collapse my left side. There's no way I can stay down and pivot through on a pitch shot.

In pitching, my three imperatives are still at work:
I still have a vertical clubface, because I know a vertical clubface is square; I'm still swinging on plane; and I keep my lag. These three things are still in play in a bunker as well.

The three imperatives are all in play here. I'm keeping my club-face square, I'm swing-ing on plane, and I'm not trying to create loft by flipping the handle—instead, I'm keeping my lag.

The 3 Imperatives – **The Full Swing**

The great thing about practicing your chipping and pitching is that you're working on your full swing at the same time, because the three essentials are consistent for all three swings. When I'm working on my chipping, I'm working on my full swing. When I'm working on my pitching, I'm working on my full swing. Even when I'm working on my putting, I'm still working on my full swing. In other words, I'm always working on my full swing. I just take my three imperatives and apply them to a fuller swing.

Face Imperative

I need to have a square clubface at address. As I swing back, I know that the face should be vertical to the ground. And I know that the face should be vertical as I swing through. Those are my three checkpoints for the full swing.

Path Imperative

I have to make sure I'm maintaining that proper swing plane. As I swing back, I can work on making sure that the club is always pointing to the target line. You can check this at every point of your swing as I'm doing in the photos below. Also notice that at key points, I flip the club in my hands so that the shaft is always a clear reference point in relation to the target line.

The divot is an important part of the path imperative. The divot is in front of the ball, because I hit the ball before I hit the ground. The divot should be going straight or slightly left, because it comes just after impact, and my club has started to turn. As I practice hitting balls, I can check my divot. I line up my clubs on the ground, then hit a couple and make sure my divots are going straight to slightly left.

Notice here that my divot is pointing slightly to the left. I've hit the ground after impact, and the club has started to turn.

Lag Imperative

The key to hitting solid iron shots is lag. You can't make a divot in front of the ball if you're trying to throw the clubhead at the ball, and that's where the lag imperative comes in. If I'm coming down and start to push the clubhead at the ball, it becomes impossible to hit the ground in front of the ball; I'm always going to be hitting the ground behind the ball. I need to know that I'm always dragging the clubhead toward impact by the handle; I'm never trying to flip the clubhead.

Think of it using this analogy: I can drag a trailer all the way from Memphis to Minneapolis going as fast as I want to go. But if I'm trying to back that trailer up, I'm not going to get to the end of the driveway without jackknifing. There's no way to push a trailer and control it, but you can pull it and control it perfectly while going as fast as you want to.

It's the same with the golf swing. If I'm using the handle to pull the clubhead through the ball, I can go as fast as I need to go and maintain control. But if I push the clubhead into the ball — jackknife.